Tactical Retirement

Strategies for Tax-Free Growth and a Safe Retirement

Cayetano (Cat) Gamboa

TDI License #1259543

Printed in the United States of America

Disclaimer

This book is presented solely for educational purposes and is not intended to represent or be used as an exhaustive financial resource. The information contained in this book is made available for illustrative purposes, explaining only the basics of investment planning.

The author and For Passion Publishing Company, LLC, emphasize this material is not offered as financial, legal, accounting, or other professional services' advice. It is highly recommended you seek the services of a competent professional before making any decisions regarding your business or personal finances.

Best efforts have underscored the writing of this book, but the author and publisher make no representations or warranties of any kind and assume no liabilities of any kind with respect to the accuracy or completeness of the contents, and specifically disclaim any implied warranties of use for any particular purpose.

Neither the author nor For Passion Publishing Company, LLC, shall be held liable or responsible to any person or entity with respect to any loss or incidental or consequential damages caused, or alleged to have been caused, directly or indirectly, by the information contained in this book, or disruption caused by errors or omissions, whether such errors or omissions result from negligence, accident, or any other cause.

The case studies and any references are fictional, and any likeness to actual persons, either living or dead, is completely coincidental. The investment case studies represented in this book were created to show only the highlights of how an investor might choose to make investment decisions.

The reader is advised to consult with a professional financial advisor who has experience with guiding clients and making investment choices relevant to an individual's financial situation.

Dedication

This book is dedicated to:

My parents, Cayetano Sr. and Evangelina Gamboa, thank you for bringing me along with 10 brothers and sisters, from Mexico to this great country. My parents taught us to work hard and get educated. Thanks to their teaching, we have stayed united and we have always tried to do the right thing and helped other people. Thank you for always believing in me and inspiring me to take on bigger challenges.

My wonderful daughter, Cathy Gamboa.

To my loving fiancé, Estibaliz Yanez, thank you for your patience, moral support, and being by my side.

I further dedicate this book to all the financial educators and other professionals with whom we have collaborated over the years so that we continually improved the services we provide our clients.

To my many loyal clients with whom I have had the opportunity and privilege of working with over the years. Thank you!

About the Author

Cayetano Gamboa is a graduate of University of Texas Pan American with a degree in Mathematics and Business. Cayetano taught mathematics for 20 years, and has been licensed to sell insurance since 1992. Cayetano is the author of Math Tactics (2008 – 2012), and Tactical Retirement (2020). Cayetano is the founder and owner of Total Retirement Solutions a successful consulting firm in South Texas.

This Book is for You if You Want to:

Preserve your wealth

Avoid high taxes

Avoid common mistakes

Stay ahead of inflation

Use interest rates to your advantage

This book reveals investment secrets
andmistakes every investor needs to know!

Total Retirement Solutions

"LET US SHOW YOU THE WAY!"

Total Retirement Solutions is a Registered Investment Advisory firm. Returns cited in this book are hypothetical examples and are not guaranteed.

We will review your current financial situation and then make recommendations about how you can increase and preserve your wealth for a safe tax-free retirement lifestyle.

Total Retirement Solutions

5401 N. Cage Blvd.

Pharr, Texas 78577

Cayetano (Cat) Gamboa

Office: (956) 685-5181

Office: (844) 827-7296

tacticalretirement@gmail.com

Table of Contents

Introduction

I have an important story to tell. It's my story about learning how to achieve financial freedom.

I can still remember walking the streets in Mexico as a six-year-old. Like most people in Mexico, we were poor. Very poor. We lived in an old small house. There were 11 of us in the family and only one bed. Our kitchen floor was dirt and we had a small outhouse for the bathroom. Our shower was the water hose that ran to the outhouse. There wasn't much to eat, and we didn't have clean clothes to wear.

A lot of the children in town were working by selling gum, shining shoes, or helping their parents sell what their parents were selling. Even as a child, I was always thinking and wondering how I could do something special to make extra money for my family.

I remember asking my mom to let me sell something. Mom always refused because either I was too young or because she felt I didn't need to do this for the family. One day I finally convinced Mom to let me sell Mexican candy. My parents made delicious Mexican candy, and they had people who would deliver the candy to different locations, or sell to the public on the street.

My father agreed with my mother that I could try, but he had very little hope of my success. My parents prepared a basket full of different kinds of candy. There was milk candy, peanuts, coconut, pumpkin and sweet potato candy. For every peso I would sell, I was going to receive and keep 35 centavos. At the young age of 6, I was on my way to earning my first peso at my first job. I was going to make my father proud of me, and I would finally have some money to spend in school.

I took my basket of candy and walked through the downtown area, to the bus station, the train station, and the park, asking everyone if they would like to buy some of my candy.

Every hour I would stop and count the money, check the leftover candy, and figure out my earnings. Somehow I miscalculated my sales and used my earnings to eat munchies, sweet water, and even some of my own merchandise.

When I returned home, my parents counted the money and they were not surprised by the results. I had eaten my entire commission and part of their merchandise. I had a deficit. I still remember Dad's smile that needed no words to explain his thoughts. I had failed at my first job. I was never allowed to sell candy again.

I had one other sales experience as a child. In a few months we were going to leave for the United States, and I remember selling oranges going door to door. One peso would buy eight oranges. Back then, 12.5 pesos equaled one US dollar. My parents had bought a truck load of oranges from the US. I never asked their permission or told them that I was taking the oranges, selling them, and keeping all the profit.

While still in Mexico I attended first and second grade. These were two very difficult years for me because I wasn't prepared to attend school. I don't remember if I knew my ABCs, but I was always good at mathematics. I was very shy, had low self-esteem, and I felt out of place.

I remember the incident that became my first footstep on the path toward becoming stronger. In our classroom, the student desks were big enough for two students. One day our teacher decided to make a new seating arrangement, and new partners were chosen randomly.

A little girl was chosen to share the desk with me. She was beautiful. She had blonde hair and was wearing a white dress with shiny white shoes. I remember sitting very quietly with a big smile, staring at her. Soon she started to cry. With tears streaming down her face, the teacher came over to find out what had happened. After a brief conversation, the teacher didn't explain anything to me, but simply moved me to the back of the room and gave the pretty girl a new partner.

How awful was I that I had made her cry? Was I that ugly or did I have a bad haircut? Were my clothes unclean or did I smell bad? It was probably all of those things. This beautiful little girl obviously came from a different world than mine. Her parents had money. She probably lived in a nice house and she knew how to pick her friends and she did not want me.

I don't blame her for crying and I don't blame her for wanting to sit with someone else. In fact, looking back now, I'm actually grateful. She taught me a good lesson, one I never forgot. I needed to figure out how not to be poor and I never wanted anybody else to ever cry again because of me.

In 1972, my parents made the best decision ever, which was to come to the United States. This was possible because my grandfather was a US citizen, and my parents were able to bring all nine children with them to the US. Two of my siblings were born in the US.

My parents were very worried, trying to figure out how to feed eleven children. My mom had several jobs as a cook at different restaurants. My dad also had several different jobs. It was a great struggle not knowing the language and not being able to read and write Spanish. We moved around a lot, from house to house, always unsettled. My parents couldn't give us much and couldn't help us in school. They left that to the schools and teachers.

This was when I decided that I wasn't going to blame my parents or my teachers if I failed. My parents couldn't help me. It was all up to me. I needed to do something so I didn't have to live in poverty.

I didn't know what to do. I didn't have a mentor. I was always a good student, especially in mathematics, and I was smart enough to go to college. After high school, I made arrangements and applied for financial aid. I told my mother about my college plans, and I still remember her every word.

"Mom, I am going to college."

"No, you're not!"

"Yes, I am."

"No, you're not! You need to find a job and help out."

"Mom, I've never listened to you before, so why should I listen to you now? I'm going to go to college. I'm going to live here, and you are going to feed me, but I am not going to ask you to help with any money."

"Okay, but you need to do good."

I was so happy she didn't slap me hard for talking to her that way! Mom believed that she had met her duty, providing me with an education until I finished high school, and now it was time for me to help out. Of course, this is very common in our culture. I don't know what my parents did right or did wrong. Whatever it was, it made me the man that I am today and I am very grateful.

After I graduated college in 1989, I got a teaching job and began teaching mathematics in high school. I taught high school math for 19 years, everything from the fundamentals of mathematics to precalculus. I realized there was no high school curriculum or math books that taught students the most important and necessary education anybody could ever receive. How does money work? How can I invest now to achieve financial independence? There was no mention of the Rule of 72. There was no information about compound interest. There was no tax education, and no one was teaching anything about the rules for investing. The school curriculum and parents failed to teach what I believed was essential for any educated person. I think the main reason this information was not and is not taught in the schools is because the teachers don't know it themselves.

Back in the early 90's, teachers had more freedom to teach the curriculum in their own way and at their own pace. Because I realized how important this information was, I modified the curriculum in my class and taught the topics I believed were most important.

In high school, freshmen in the lower math class were learning useless information, like multiplying three-digit numbers by three-digit numbers. There was too much room for error and this is something any calculator could do. I decided to stop using the classroom books and curriculum and instead I began to teach my students algebra. My teaching methods were simple to understand, and my students could follow my instruction. My students were more successful than in other classrooms, and they were well-prepared for the next year's curriculum. Since I was having success, I implemented my own plan to teach my students about the Rule of 72 and how money works.

I also explained how banks operate, and how they use the Rule of 72 to multiply their money. I developed my own quizzes and curriculum, and began teaching about investing early, the difference between variable accounts and fixed accounts, and other important rules about investing. My students were 15 to17-year-olds and they probably didn't do much with what they learned, but I was trying to teach them what I knew and what I considered to be the most important lesson they could learn. This curriculum was not available from any other teacher in our school or anywhere else as far as I knew. I also knew that my students would never get this information from their parents, because their parents also did not understand how to work with money.

In the early 90's I got licensed with Primerica, a financial service company whose main teaching was buying term and investing the difference. That adventure didn't last long. During my school years, the only investments I knew about were fixed annuities that yielded around 3%, variable annuities, and mutual funds. Many of my teacher coworkers were opening 403(b)s using fixed interest rate accounts. They were afraid of mutual funds and any other investments in the market.

I remember when one of my closest friends was retiring and he was getting ready to withdraw money from his Teacher Retirement System account to invest the money in an annuity. The licensed agent he spoke with used fear tactics to convince my friend to open a fixed interest rate account instead of other investment options. At the time I didn't know much, but I did know that fixed annuities were not capable of beating inflation. According to what I knew and what I was teaching my students, fixed annuities were considered bad investments. Fixed indexed annuities were already available, and it took a long time for fixed annuities to become popular.

Over the years, I kept seeing the same thing. The few teachers who were investing to supplement their retirement were using the wrong accounts. Teachers were making too many mistakes. I realized then that students were not the only ones who needed help. What could I do differently? How could I make a difference?

This is when I began to learn more about investing and about the power of insurance policies to secure and increase wealth. I took courses, I read everything I could get my hands on, and before long I started to use my license again.

In this book you will learn many secrets about money and how money works. The book will also reveal mistakes that people are making and topics that no one talks about: taxes, social security, the bad TRS system, and the controversial income rider.

You will learn the importance of investing in a tax-free investment so you can avoid paying taxes completely. I also discuss 401(k)s, traditional and Roth IRAs, and introduce Indexed Universal Life (IUL) insurance as possibly the most effective investment tool ever created.

When you finish reading this book, you will find my offer to provide you with a free financial review so you can assess your current situation and find out how to improve your circumstances. I guarantee I will find at least two ways to help you make more money, more safely.

I appreciate your interest in learning about your financial strength and well-being, and I assure you that my staff and I are here to assist you in any way we can because it is our pride and joy to help families achieve a financially secure tax-free life.

We are at your service!

Best wishes,

Cayetano (Cat) Gamboa.

Chapter 1
The Danger of Taxes

It's been said that taxes are a necessary evil. Nobody likes taxes because they eat away at our wealth, yet they also fund important services that we and our families rely upon such as schools, hospitals, highways, fire departments, law enforcement and other socially important parts of our daily lives.

> "I like to pay taxes. With them, I buy civilization."
> Oliver Wendell Holmes, Jr.

Even so, taxes are still a danger to building your wealth, steadily eating away at the achievement of your financial goals. When people are asked to identify the largest expense in their lives, most people think of their home or medical expenses, but it might surprise you to know that the biggest expense is the money you pay in taxes. This is true even today when we're near the LOWEST tax rates EVER in modern history.

One thing you can always count on, besides death and taxes, is that the tax rate is going to change, sooner or later. This means that when you are planning your financial future, you have to be ready for unwelcome and frightening changes that could affect your retirement.

No one can predict what our nation's financial circumstances will be in 20, 30, or 40 years, but it's important you know:

1. The current tax levels will not stay the same,
2. Your future plans for retirement could be seriously affected, and
3. Careful thought must be given today to planning your financial security in the unknown future.

The History of U.S. Taxes

Don't worry, this is not going to be a lengthy history presentation! However, there are several interesting facts you need to know. You're welcome to do research on your own, of course, but in the meantime, here is some important information. Take this information with a grain of salt because this is simply an overview to convey the main idea that tax rates can change when it suits the political party in power who believe they can make these changes without losing votes that costs them their jobs.

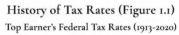

History of Tax Rates (Figure 1.1)
Top Earner's Federal Tax Rates (1913-2020)

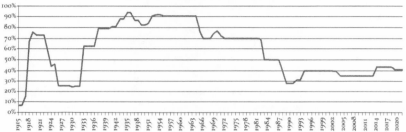

1. The Civil War: The first income tax was created in 1861.
2. World War 1: In 1916, the tax rate jumped from 16% to 67%, then to 77% in 1918.
3. The Depression: The tax rate was changed from 25% to 63%.
4. World War II: In 1944 it peaked at 94%.
5. In the 1950s, 1960s and 1970s it never dipped below 70%.
6. In the 1980s it was reduced from 70% to 50% then to 28%.
7. From the 1990s to 2018, the rate has been up and down from 35% to 43%.
8. Donald Trump lowered the rate for top earners from 40.8% to 37%.

Today, the highest income tax rate is 37%, and it was lowered from 40.8%; this tax rate is in effect from 2018 – December 2025, and then this tax rate expires.

The history of taxes is important. It shows that the tax rates and the tax laws are always changing. These changes will affect you and will influence your investment portfolio. A war is not required for taxes to go up. We have other issues that are affecting our economy right now, things like our nation's deficit, the Baby Boomers, and the Coronavirus that came out of nowhere.

Why Are Taxes Going Up Soon?

Two of the three biggest expenses of the federal government are Social Security, and healthcare. It's very easy to see what's happening right now. Every day more than 10,000 seniors from the Baby Boomer generation are turning 65. That's every day all year long...for the next 11 years! That's 300,000 Baby Boomers every month. That's 3,600,000 Baby Boomers every year... 39,600,000 between now and 2030. Who do you think is paying for those Social Security and Medicare benefits?

People are receiving substantial government benefits for the first time in their lives, adding more burden to the nation's responsibilities and a whole lot more debt.

The primary revenue sources to pay for these huge expenses are income tax and payroll tax. Frankly, payroll tax will not be enough. That means your taxes are going up!

Our Nation's Debt

Another cause for concern is the tremendous amount of debt our country already holds. Bill Clinton was the only president since John F. Kennedy to actually decrease the deficit. All other presidents added to the budget deficit. Under President Obama, the national debt doubled from $10.6 trillion to almost $20 trillion when he left in 2016.

The increase of almost $10 trillion is blamed on the tremendous cost of our country's wars in Iraq and Afghanistan, the Baby Boomers and the Great Recession that President Bush left behind. Our military spending is the highest in the world, almost more than three times the world's second biggest military spender, the People's Republic of China.

President Trump promised he would fix our nation's debt problem, but instead, in February 2020, our national debt rose to $23 trillion, the largest government debt in the world. That was before COVID-19. That's also when President Trump signed a $1.5 trillion tax cut that lowered the top corporate tax rate from 35% to 21%, giving corporations a tax break. Every tax break creates more debt for our nation.

The point is that our government is increasing its already massive debts and for the country to stay on its feet and not collapse, Congress is likely to come knocking on your door and telling you, not asking, telling you that you have to start paying higher taxes.

The United States made a tremendous mistake staying in debt when our economy was so strong, but that's the reality, and spending can't stop now because the government is trying to rescue our economy from the greatest shock it has ever felt since the Great Depression, the Coronavirus.

COVID-19

The deadly Coronavirus that came from China in late 2019 has taken the world community by fear, as deaths increased quickly and world leaders struggled to contain the epidemic. The timing was awful because the market was high and employment was low. In just a few days, the markets lost more than 30% of their value. People were forced to stay home and the economy stopped. When the Coronavirus epidemic began, the Treasury Department suddenly had to borrow another $3 trillion to help Americans who had to close their businesses or were unemployed, and to restart the economy. Apparently, this is not the end of this economic nightmare as more trillions of dollars will be needed to help our economy after shutting down for so long.

Over 22 million Americans have filed for unemployment and many of these people will never get their old jobs back. Families are lining up at food banks for the first time ever in their lives as they wait for unemployment checks to help them pay for rent, food, insurance and all the other regular expenses.

The government wants you to think that everything will be okay, but the reality is that many people will not have any jobs to go back to and many businesses that were surviving from month-to-month will never be able to reopen their doors. Period.

The Coronavirus pandemic has hurt our national economy tremendously. According to economists, the United States must continue adding to its debt to avoid an economic depression or there won't be enough of an economy left to pay back the debt once this health crisis is over. Our national economy is in very serious trouble.

There are only two ways to lower the federal debt. One choice is to spend less, and the other is to raise taxes. It's pretty clear that we're not going to be able to stop spending. The government may need to spend more and more money to find ways to rescue the economy, and that means the government's only solution is to increase taxes. Your taxes.

Newly released budget estimates are projecting that the fiscal 2021 deficit will reach $2.1 trillion in 2021, and average $1.3 trillion through 2025 as the economy recovers from the damage caused by Coronavirus-related shutdowns.

Taxes in the Future

Something else to remember is that the recently passed Tax Cuts and Jobs Act (TCJA) signed into law by President Trump in December 2017, is set to expire in December 2025. This law provided the temporary reduction of individual income tax rates, and its time is almost over, meaning an end to the current lower tax rates. Do you think this will be a good opportunity for a tax increase?

No one knows for certain what the future will bring. Yet, there are indications that change is coming soon. Taxes are the way the federal government raises money to pay for its expenditures which include very big obligations like military defense, Social Security, Medicare and Medicaid, and paying interest on the federal debt which is somewhere near $23 trillion. The United States has an aging population which means that the expenses for Social Security and Medicare are going up, up, up.

In 2008, David Walker, the former U.S. Comptroller General, told Congress it would have to double taxes to make ends meet. Today in 2020, that would be a start, not a solution.

The SECURE Act of 2019

There is yet another danger lurking that you should know about and avoid. In December 2019, Congress passed the SECURE Act which included new guidelines about inherited IRAs. If you inherit a retirement plan such as an IRA, or you are a non-spouse beneficiary on a 401(k), the old rules allowed you to withdraw from that retirement account for the rest of your life.

Now, going forward, you must take all your distributions within a 10-year period. This means you are forced to pay your taxes sooner. What tax rate will you have to pay? Because of this shorter timeframe, people who saved money in their 401(k)s or IRAs might need to reconsider their situation and come up with a new tax strategy to avoid paying too much in taxes now.

What will you do?

The point of this information is to strongly suggest that you need to carefully plan for your financial future now and protect the wealth you've built from being swallowed by the tax tsunami heading your way.

The time to act is right now. The good news is that this book will show you a number of strategies you can use to create a tax-free retirement and preserve your wealth.

Summary

The lessons learned in this chapter are:

1. Taxes and tax codes don't stay the same forever.
2. The federal government's debts are increasing to a point where obligations to Social Security, Medicare and the economy may limit the government's ability to support other important programs.
3. Because of this increasing financial stress, there is a strong likelihood that your taxes are going to increase in the near future.
4. It's important you recognize the need to review your retirement investment strategy NOW and make the necessary changes, revealed shortly in this book, so you can maximize your investments tax-free for a safe, secure retirement lifestyle.

Chapter 2
Social Security Won't Be Enough

When should I collect my benefits? This is a very important decision. Most people should study their present and future finances when making this decision. Other important factors are penalties for continuing to work and, of course, taxes.

For all or most of your working life you contributed to the Social Security system. Each month your employer legally withheld part of your earnings as a way of collecting your federal income tax, and then funneled your tax money to a variety of programs, two of which were Social Security and Medicare. Now that you're getting closer to retirement, the funds set aside in your Social Security account all these years will soon be available for you. When should I collect?

It may be hard to believe, but 94% of the people on Social Security started receiving their benefits at the wrong time. You have the opportunity to be one of the 6% who get it right!

Social Security Only Funds Part of What You Will Need

The Social Security program used to be called the federal Old-Age, Survivors, and Disability Insurance program (OASDI). This program was created to help people supplement their retirement, and it was never intended to be the only source of retirement income. The money you can expect to receive will only be a portion of what you are likely to need during your retirement years.

Unfortunately, for 66% of all retirees, the Social Security check is the ONLY check they receive. In 2018, the average monthly Social Security check was $1,400, which is $16,800 per year before taxes. For a retiree who is still paying a mortgage, or must pay rent, medical bills, food and utilities, this is simply not enough. Many seniors will not have enough money and will be a burden to their families or the government.

What Is Your Full Retirement Age (FRA)?

The first question to answer when considering when to start your social security benefits is "What is my full retirement age (FRA)?" This is to determine the amount of money you will receive monthly if you start early, or how much you would receive if you waited until your FRA.

Study the chart below to determine your FRA:

Full Retirement Age and Year of Birth (Figure 2.1)

Age to receive full Social Security benefits	
Year of birth	Full retirement age
1943-1954	66
1955	66 and 2 months
1956	66 and 4 months
1957	66 and 6 months
1958	66 and 8 months
1959	66 and 10 months
1960 and later	67
NOTE: People born on January 1 of any year, refer to the previous year.	

As you can see, the chart above helps you determine when you will be eligible for Full Retirement Age benefits. There are 96 months during which you could file for Social Security benefits between the ages of 62 - 70, and any month you select will result in a different benefit amount. This is why it's so important to carefully choose the best time to initiate your benefits. If you get your benefits too soon, you will lose money you might otherwise receive.

The amount of money you receive from Social Security is based on the number of years you contributed to the Social Security program, and also the amount of money you contributed each year. The chart below is based on an assumed benefit of $1,000 at the full retirement age of 66. The benefits change depending on when you initiate your benefits.

Monthly Benefit Amount Based on Claiming (Figure 2.2)

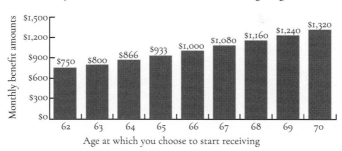

A Case Study

Let's take a look at a case study for an imaginary retiree named Mark. Mark's FRA is age 66 and he is entitled to $1,000 monthly. If Mark started receiving his benefits at 62 years old, he would only receive 75% of what he could have, just $750, which is a very large decrease (-25%) from the potential Mark would otherwise receive if he waits. He would receive $36,000 ($750 x 12 months x 4 years) before he turns 66.

Let's take a closer look at this example and see what happens by the time Mark reaches age 78. Mark is receiving $750 per month x 12 months per year x 16 years to age 78. Here is the calculation: $750 x 12 months x 16 years = $144,000.

If Mark had waited to age 66, which is his FRA, he would receive $1,000 each month. At age 78 he would have received the same amount of money in 12 years instead of 16 years: $1,000 x 12 months x 12 years = $144.000.

Age 78 is the breakeven point when the money Mark received by starting early at age 62 is roughly the same as the money Mark received by starting his benefits at age 66. But then, after age 78, Mark receives $250 more each month for the rest of his life because he delayed his benefits by four years and waited until his FRA. Take a look at the following chart:

Comparison of Break-Even Points for Initial Distribution (Figure 2.3)

Age	Start at age 62 Monthly Benefit $750	Start at age 66 Monthly Benefit $1,000	Start at age 70 Monthly Benefit $1,320
62	$ 9,000		
63	$ 18,000		
64	$ 27,000		
65	$ 36,000		
66	$ 45,000	$ 12,000	
67	$ 54,000	$ 24,000	
68	$ 63,000	$ 36,000	
69	$ 72,000	$ 48,000	
70	$ 81,000	$ 60,000	$ 15,840
71	$ 90,000	$ 72,000	$ 31,680
72	$ 99,000	$ 84,000	$ 47,520
73	$ 108,000	$ 96,000	$ 63,360
74	$ 117,000	$ 108,000	$ 79,200
75	$ 126,000	$ 120,000	$ 95,040
76	$ 135,000	$ 132,000	$ 110,880
77	$ 144,000	$ 144,000	$ 126,720
78	$ 153,000	$ 156,000	$ 142,560
79	$ 162,000	$ 168,000	$ 158,400
80	$ 171,000	$ 180,000	$ 174,240
81	$ 180,000	$ 192,000	$ 190,080
82	$ 189,000	$ 204,000	$ 205,920
83	$ 198,000	$ 216,000	$ 221,760
84	$ 207,000	$ 228,000	$ 237,600
85	$ 216,000	$ 240,000	$ 253,440

Break-even point · More income after 78 · Break-even point · More income after 82

By looking at the chart, you can also see that if Mark delayed taking his benefits until he was 70 years old, by age 82 he would be receiving more benefits than if he started at age 66, (32% more) and much more than if he started receiving benefits at age 62.

Social Security offers a variety of monthly benefit amounts depending on when you initiate your benefits, and there are several strategies you must consider which might make your retirement lifestyle more secure and comfortable. A good idea, right?

When Should I Begin Receiving Benefits?

Remember that for 66% of the beneficiaries, Social Security is the only check they receive and they cannot wait for their FRA. They must take a reduced amount right away. Other people believe they won't live that long, so they want to start receiving their benefits as soon as possible.

I still remember my dad in the early 1990s talking about applying for Social Security at age 62. He looked excited thinking that Social Security was going to take care of him. The look on his face said it all when he found out the tiny amount he was going to receive. He contributed to Social Security for only 20 years and his earnings per year were not much. Even if I had suggested he wait until 65, he had his reasons to get it at age 62.

The answer of when to start is different for everyone. It's an individual choice, and it is based on each person's unique circumstances. There might be a big problem like a serious illness or injury, a job loss, or a lack of savings. Other taxpayers may choose to wait to receive their benefits because they are still working or they have sufficient resources and can afford to delay their benefits until they are 70. There are many different situations. Either way, Social Security is such an important part of your retirement income that you should make a serious effort to carefully consider your options and then make the best choice that's right for your unique circumstances.

The Penalties for Working While Receiving Benefits: Some people choose to start their benefits and keep working at the same time, but you should know that benefits will be reduced or even eliminated during the months when you are working.

Example of Benefits Before, At, and After FRA (Figure 2.4)

Younger than Full Retirement Age	In the year you reach Full Retirement Age	Older than Full Retirement Age
You can earn up to $18,240	You can earn up to $48,600	No earnings limit
After this point, your benefits will be reduced by $1 for every $2 you earn over the limit	After this point, your benefits will be reduced by $1 for every $3 you earn over the limit	No reduction in benefits

If you are younger than full retirement age (FRA), you will receive $1 less in benefits for every $2 you earn above $18,240. When you reach your Full Retirement Age, your benefits will be reduced $1 for every $3 you earn over $48,000. Once you are older than your Full Retirement Age, you no longer pay a penalty and can work and earn as much as you want and still receive your full Social Security retirement benefit.

Taxes on Social Security

Many people want to know if they have to pay taxes on the Social Security benefits they receive, and the answer is... maybe, maybe not.

Taxes on Social Security Benefits (Figure 2.5)

Tax filing status	Provisional income	Percentage of your benefits that may be taxable
Single or Head of Household	less than $25,000	None
Single or Head of Household	between $25,000 and $34,000	up to 50%
Single or Head of Household	more than $34,000	up to 85%
Married Filing Jointly	less than $32,000	None
Married Filing Jointly	between $32,000 and $44,000	up to 50%
Married Filing Jointly	more than $44,000	up to 85%

Once again, it's a matter of your individual circumstances. It all depends on how much income you have. If your provisional income is more than $34,000, it's likely that you will pay taxes of up to 85% of your Social Security benefits.

Married couples who file jointly will pay taxes on about 50% of their Social Security income if their provisional income is between $32,000 and $44,000. When income is greater than $44,000, 85% is taxable.

This is very important to note: Receiving money from accounts like Roth IRAs or IULs is not considered provisional income. This means your distributions won't be taxed because you already paid the tax when you originally made your contributions. So again, having Roth or IUL accounts bring big benefits.

Benefits of Staying at Your Job Longer:

- No tax penalties for continuing to work after FRA
- Health insurance at work (You don't receive Medicare until age 65)
- Higher contributions into Social Security, therefore higher benefits
- Continue to contribute to your 401k or IRA

Caution: Remember, Social Security was never meant to be your only source of income during retirement. It was meant to supplement other accounts like a pension, a 401(k), IRAs, or a cash value life insurance policy. Most people need help with planning and investing for their retirement. It just makes good sense to receive the advice of a financial professional who can evaluate your circumstances, provide you with different choices, and help you consider which is the best one for you and your family.

Summary

The lessons learned in this chapter are:

1. Social Security will only fund part of what you need in retirement.
2. Delaying your benefits until after your FRA may bring you greater benefits for life.
3. If you decide to work while receiving your Social Security benefits, benefits could be reduced or even eliminated during the months when you are working.
4. Depending on your income, you may, or may not, have to pay taxes on your Social Security benefits.
5. It makes sense to speak with a professional who is familiar with Social Security issues and can give you a clear understanding of your choices so you can make the best choice for you and your family.

Chapter 3
Using the Rule of 72 to Build Your Wealth

Money.

How does it work? If you asked this question of most people, they wouldn't know how to answer. I once asked my friend and he said, "Yes, of course I do. I earn it and my wives spend it." It is funny that money is what most people work for and live for, and money is what many believe buys happiness, and yet we know so little about how it works.

On a typical Sunday morning, John, Danny and I usually play golf. We bet on every hole from 25 cents to $5 per bet depending on the situation. All for fun. To add to the story, all three of us were math teachers at one time. On the first tee box, we usually agree on what we are going to bet. This time I suggested to start the bet at 10 cents and double the bet on every hole. Both looked at me and started to laugh. "Let's play for real money," they said. I insisted, and allowed that anybody who wanted to quit betting at any time could quit.

Everything was good for the first six holes. After the 7th hole, there were questions and concerns because they figured out that the bet was more than what anybody could afford. We stopped betting after the 6th hole.

18-Holes of Golf, Doubling the Bet After Every Hole (Figure 3.1)

1	$0.10		7	$6.40		13	$409.60
2	$0.20		8	$12.80		14	$819.20
3	$0.40		9	$25.60		15	$1,638.40
4	$0.80		10	$51.20		16	$3,276.80
5	$1.60		11	$102.40		17	$6,553.60
6	$3.20		12	$204.80		18	13,107.20

It is amazing how compounding works. Given enough time, even small amounts can easily multiply to amazing results.

Because money is such an important part of our daily lives, and because we rely upon it for a safe and comfortable future, everyone should be educated about how to use money to their advantage.

Let's learn about the most important rule everyone should follow. This important rule is called the Rule of 72. The Rule of 72 is a method for calculating how long it will take for an investment, or a debt, to double in value. This rule is considered a "rule of thumb" for making a fairly accurate estimate. Everybody works for money. Let's learn how money works for us.

The way it works is like this: divide the number 72 by the percentage you expect to earn. The result will tell you approximately how many years it will take for your investment to double. The Rule of 72 is based on the mathematics of the steady addition of compound interest adding to the value of your account over time until it doubles.

When you invest your money, you receive interest on that money, and the interest also earns interest. This is called compound interest. Compound interest is also known as "interest on interest".

Here's an example. Let's suppose that a 29-year-old person named Alice is going to invest $10,000. Her investment will return 4%. As you can see from the illustration below, it will take Alice's investment of $10,000 18 years to double and become $20,000 at age 47. If Alice does not withdraw any money and her account continues to earn 4% per year, in another 18 years when Alice is 65 years old, the $20,000 will double again and become $40,000.

Alice's $10,000 at 4%.

$$72/4\% = 18 \text{ years}$$

Age	4%
29	$10,000
47	$20,000
65	$40,000

Now consider what happens when the 29-year-old Alice takes the same $10,000 but invests this money at an 8% rate of return. When we divide 72 by 8, we learn it will take nine years for this money to double. This means Alice's $10,000 will double every nine years at 8%.

Here's an interesting question to think about. Alice chose an interest rate that was double...from 4% to 8%. Will her money double over the same time period as well? She is, after all, investing her money at double the interest rate, so it seems to make sense that her money will double, too.

Let's see how this works out over time: At age 29, Alice invested $10,000 at an 8% rate of return. Nine years later when Alice is 38, she has $20,000. Nine years later the money has doubled to $40,000 when Alice is 47. The money will double again to $80,000 at age 56., and double again to $160,000 when Alice is 65.

Alice's Money at 4%, and 8%.

72/8% = 18 years

72/4% = 18 years

Age	4%
29	$10,000
47	$20,000
65	$40,000

Age	8%
29	$10,000
38	$20,000
47	$40,000
56	$80,000
65	$160,000

As you can see from the comparison of the two charts, Alice's money did not double over the course of the 36 years. Her money quadrupled and is now worth four times more than the money she invested at 4%.

By quadrupling her money, instead of $80,000 Alice has $160,000. This is the power of compound interest and it illustrates how the Rule of 72 works.

Now consider what would happen if Alice invested her money at 12%.

Imagine the results if Alice invested her money at 18%. The original $10,000 invested at 12% compounds to $640,000 over the same period of time. At 18%, Alice is a multimillionaire with $5,120,000. This is the magic of compound interest.

We learn two important points of information from these examples. First, the Rule of 72 illustrates the importance of investing over time. Secondly, increasing the investment percentage makes a big difference on the outcome. Simply investing at 1% more will result in thousands of dollars more in interest. So, bottom line, the earlier a person starts their investment, the more time there is for the money to compound. It's also very clear that earning a higher interest rate over time will make a gigantic difference in the sum.

There was once a very smart guy who said, "Compound interest is the eighth wonder of the world". The person was none other than Albert Einstein. Einstein also said, "He who understands it, earns it; he who doesn't, pays it." When Einstein said the phrase "understands it", he meant "applies it".

We can all agree that Albert Einstein was one of the most brilliant scientists of our time, so it's worth noting that he also said, "There is no force in the universe more powerful than compound interest", and he called it "mankind's greatest invention".

Once you understand the power of the Rule of 72 and how compound interest is a miraculous multiplier of your wealth, the next step is to implement this rule and use it to your own financial advantage so you maximize your investments.

It's important to recognize there are bad investments and good investments, as well as bad debt and good debt. By recognizing and understanding these four kinds of situations, you'll be in a good position to find better alternatives so compound interest can be your friend, not your enemy.

Bad Debt

Compound interest is an amazing tool that can be your best friend when its power is working with you and helping you increase your wealth, but it can also be your worst enemy when you have debt and its power is working against you.

Any debt over 6% is considered a bad debt to most people. Remember what Einstein said about compound interest. To paraphrase, "He who doesn't understand it, pays it."

Banks and credit card companies love to extend credit because they are making billions of dollars on interest from people who are trapped in debt. Some people are paying credit card interest as high as 28% and only paying monthly minimums. This is a trap that's very difficult to escape.

Other people have personal loans at a cost of 8% or higher. Some people with bad credit obtain bad car loans, or they get self-financed mortgage loans with high interest rates. These are bad debts because the interest paid on the borrowed money is too high.

The best advice you'll ever hear is to pay-off these debts as fast as possible because they are devastating your opportunity to build wealth for yourself. Make an extra payment or get a loan consolidation, or even get an extra job because if these debts are not eliminated, you are destroying your retirement plans.

Bad Investments

You'd be amazed to find out how many people have savings that are yielding only 1% - 3%. These people mistakenly believe that a savings account or a money market account is an investment. These are not investments; they are just parking spaces to hold cash for short-term use. Certificate of Deposits (CDs) yield about 1% - 2%, and money market accounts yield about 2%. Currently, bonds are also at historically low interest rates. You can't protect your money at these low rates. Using the Rule of 72 divided by 2%, and it will take at least 36 years for these accounts to double. Most of us would be dead and will never see it happen.

Most of these accounts aren't even earning enough to beat inflation, which averages around 3% per year. This means that people are losing their buying power by keeping their money in these kinds of accounts. There's no point keeping your money in an account that's losing value, especially when you have a great opportunity to invest your money in an investment vehicle that can earn solid gains.

People who are saving money in these accounts don't understand the effect inflation is having on their money. Also, many of these people are afraid of other types of fixed investments such as annuities. Banks and credit card companies take advantage of this and use the FDIC guarantee of ensuring deposits to prey upon people's fears so people stay away from other investments. FDIC insured accounts include checking, savings, trust, certificates of deposit (CDs), and money market deposit accounts.

When your money is in these accounts, you are earning the bare minimum for your money. It's the banks and insurance companies who are making huge amounts of money, and using your money to do it. It's very important to change the way you think about money, and find ways where you can invest and earn at least 7% - 8% per year.

Later in this book I'll explain how you can be your own bank so you can borrow inexpensive money and use it to make more money for yourself. This way you'll have good investments and good debt, borrowing cheap money to make more money for yourself just like the banks do.

As you remember, I've been a mathematics teacher and I have never seen the amazing Rule of 72 in any high school or college math book. This rule is not commonly known, but I think you can see how important it is and how it can be used to tremendous advantage.

The philosophy of our culture is that young people should go to college, study hard, and learn the skills that will get them a good job so they can earn money and have a happy life. Yet, our educational system does not teach our youth the fundamentals of financial education so they can secure a decent and comfortable future.

Our students need to learn how compound interest works. They need to learn how to find and invest in a strong investment vehicle, and to do so when they are young. The youth of our country also need to know how to avoid getting in debt and how to manage their dangerous credit cards.

It's very unfortunate that teachers and parents don't teach their students and children how to invest money, or how to avoid debt. One of the first things high school students do when they attend college is take out student loans and apply for credit cards. Banks and credit card companies expect this behavior and they deliberately target the young. Sadly, students are their best customers and most students who fall into debt usually stay in debt. They are living on credit, paying off debt ineffectively, and destroying their financial future.

Because of this lack of education, we now have a society with many financial illiterates. The young people in our country today do not have sufficient knowledge about how to properly use money to their advantage, and they are not prepared to face the obstacles and dangers that await them.

This book, Tactical Retirement, explains one of the best financial strategies available today, and can educate both young and mature adults to overcome the financial problems they face.

Now is the time to teach our children the information they need and get them started by opening up a good investment account early in life. The sooner we do this, the sooner our children will understand and start down the road toward their financial success.

Summary

The lessons learned in this chapter are:

1. Compound interest is your best friend or your worst enemy.
2. The Rule of 72 helps you understand how to calculate the time it will take for your money to double.

3. Every additional interest rate percentage makes a big difference to your investment results.
4. The sooner you invest, the more time your money has to grow.
5. Albert Einstein, probably the smartest person ever born, considered compounding the eighth wonder of the world.
6. Keeping your money in very low interest rate accounts such as bank savings accounts, money market accounts or CDs is destroying the purchasing power of your money.
7. Banks and insurance companies borrow your money, pay you very low interest, and use your money to make more money for themselves.
8. Staying in debt and paying high interest rates is devastating your investment time and your investment potential.
9. The school system has failed to teach financial education, and most of the people in our country lack financial literacy and don't understand how money can work to their advantage.
10. This book, Tactical Retirement, offers a tremendous advantage by explaining one of the best financial strategies available today.

Chapter 4
Tax-Deferred Wealth in Your 401(k) and IRAs

Are you one of those fortunate people who happen to have a pension or a 401(k) at work? Great, but you are not in the clear. These are all taxable accounts and you have more than just future taxes to worry about.

The most common types of retirement accounts are 401(k)s, 403(b)s, IRAs, Simple IRAs, and pensions. These accounts are all tax-deferred accounts. They provide an upfront tax break when you make a deposit and you pay taxes when you withdraw your money in retirement—so the tax is "deferred". These accounts are not bad but they are not considered the best, either. Here is a list of five investment accounts listed from best to worst. This is the order that I believe smart investments should follow and not skip over the smarter options.

Tax-Deferred Account Rankings (Figure 4.1)

FREE MONEY	TAX FREE	TAX DEFERRED	TAXABLE MONEY	NON-DEFERRED
401K - Pensions 403b (some)	Roth IRA IUL	Non-qualified Investment	IRA, 403b, 401k - Pensions Social Security	Bank CDs Money Market
Employer % Contribution Tax Deferred All Taxable	After Tax Money Not Taxable	After Tax Money Tax Deferred Taxable Interest	Before Tax Money Tax Deferred All Taxable	After Tax Money Not Deferred Taxable Interest

401(k)s and Pensions

Free Money is number one on the list. If you already have either a company 401(k), or a company pension, you are fortunate.

With a 401(k) or a pension, the employer contributes funds into the account. In other words, this is FREE money and free money is the best money there is. The employer matches about 3% to 6% of the employee's salary. Some pensions are 100% fully funded by the employer, while other pensions match the employee contributions which are set by the employer. Some employers offer both a 401(k) and a pension but this situation diminishes every day. Either way, make sure you invest enough in your 401(k) to get the maximum benefit of the company matching funds (free money). Many employees contribute more than what the company matches and overfund their 401(k) because it's tax-deferred funds, though not the best investment, at least start you in the right direction. Employees with 401(k)s can contribute up to $19,500 in 2020. Anyone age 50 or over is eligible for an additional catch-up contribution of $6,500 in 2020 for a total annual contribution of $26,000...all of it tax-deferred.

Those who contribute outside their 401(k) usually contribute into a traditional IRA. Both of these accounts are deferred and considered Taxable Money after the distribution phase starts during retirement. These accounts jumped from the best in the list (Free Money), to fourth in the list (Taxable Money), which are not considered the best choice. If you are contributing more than what the company is matching into your 401(k) and also have an IRA, stop. Your objective is to get as much Free Money as possible and maximize the second in the list Tax-Free Money. Why is Tax-Free the second on the list? Because it is tax-free.

Your 403(b) Account

A 403(b) is a tax-advantaged retirement account for employees of nonprofit organizations or tax-exempt organizations such as schools, hospitals, government employees and librarians. It's very similar to a 401(k). The same level of contributions applies: $19,500 in 2020 and catch-up contributions of $6,500. Tax is also deferred and considered taxable money when distribution starts in retirement. The biggest and most important difference is that most non-profit employers **don't match** contributions in the 403(b). If your company is not providing matching contributions, then why even start one of these accounts when there are definitely better options out there?

Many nonprofit organizations offer pensions to their employees but employees need another account to help employees supplement lost income gaps at retirement.

In the 1990s, as a math teacher, I remember when insurance agents would attend our school and offer 403(b)s. They would set up a table, bring cookies and the office staff would make an announcement for the faculty and staff to stop by and visit.

These agents could only offer 403(b)s through either annuities or mutual funds, and they were hoping to transfer your old account into a new one. The agents were only allowed to offer 403(b)s, and were not able to offer Tax-Free accounts like Roth IRAs nor IULs.

Teachers not only receive a bad pension but they also have the worst options for retirement with the 403(b). This account has severe restrictions when it comes to withdrawal or transfers. If you have a 403(b), stop contributing and open a Tax-Free account. Please read Chapter 8, which is for teachers.

Simple IRA and Traditional IRAs

A SIMPLE IRA is an excellent tool that allows small business owners to help their employees save for retirement. This type of retirement account combines the features of the traditional IRA with the features of the 401(k). The SIMPLE IRA is subject to annual contribution limits of $13,500. This is higher than the $6,000 annual limit for traditional and Roth IRAs, but less than the limit for 401(k)s. Both the Simple IRA and traditional IRA also contribute pre-tax dollars and defers taxes until you start your distributions.

All of these accounts, the 401(k)s, 403(b)s, and IRAs, will eventually add to the tax burden that is coming and that we are trying to avoid. If we know that we will have a tax problem in the future, why don't we try to fix it right now? If you had a leaky roof or faucet, will you wait until the problem gets worse and more costly or would you call the roofer or plumber right away? We would all try minimize the damage, and pay now rather than later. We should do the same with taxes...pay now rather than later.

Non-Qualified Accounts

A non-qualified account is what I call tax-deferred, even though most of the others are also tax deferred. In these accounts we use after-tax money. The contribution amount is not taxable, but the interest earned by the account is taxable. For example, Liz invests $100,000 of after-tax money from her bank account into an annuity. Ten years later her annuity is worth $180,000. Only the $80,000 is taxable, not the original $100,000. To avoid having the interest taxed, individuals with these accounts should open a tax-free account like a Roth or an IUL instead.

Not Deferred and Taxable

Bank CDs and Certificate of Deposit are not even considered investments. The little interest they yield is not even deferred. Taxes on the earnings are paid right away. These savings accounts don't even beat inflation, which averages 3% per year. People with these types of accounts are making the banks rich and need serious financial education because they are letting the value of their money erode...safely going broke. Many individuals have hundreds of thousands of dollars in CDs for inheritance and should consider every other option. Almost any other account would give better results.

What should I do?

All 401(k)s, 403(b)s, IRAs, and pensions are taxable deferred accounts. The best objective is to follow the chart from most favorable to least favorable, putting your money in the type of accounts that are best for you. This should be your plan.

A combination of taxable and tax-free accounts is recommended. A tax-free account like a Roth or an IUL should complement your other accounts.

Free money is first. If you are fortunate to have an account with an employer who contributes to your retirement account, take advantage of this excellent opportunity. These accounts are 401(k)s, pensions, some 403(b)s and most Simple IRAs. Invest in the account just enough to maximize the company's matching percentage. Usually the company matches at between 3% to 6%, but rarely more. All additional monies should be placed into a Tax-Free Money account, which is second on the list. These accounts are Roth IRAs and Index Universal Life Insurance (IUL). These are after-tax accounts so their accumulation and growth are never taxed again. When taxes go up in the future, your accounts will be free from taxation.

Roth IRA or a Traditional IRA

The million-dollar question is "Which is better? A Roth IRA or taxable accounts like a 401(k) or traditional IRA?" Many argue that if the tax rate stays the same, it should not matter whether you pay taxes now or later. Let's look at the next chart.

Comparison of a Taxable Account and a Tax-Deferred Account (Figure 4.2)

$1,000 (Pay Now)	$1,000 (Pay Later)
-$200 (Taxed 20%)	-$0 (NO taxes)
$800 Invested	$1,000 Invested
10 years	10 years
6% Interest Rate	6% Interest Rate
$1,432.68	$1,790.85
No More Taxes	20% Taxes
$1,432.68	$1,432.68

The chart above illustrates a $1,000 investment taxed at 20% with the same time period and at the same rate of return. As you can see, if taxes stay the same, the total results are exactly the same. The math is correct. They are correct. But what most advisors don't mention and fail to explain is that having a combination of both taxable and non-taxable accounts helps reduce taxes. The chart below uses the current tax rates.

This example is of a couple who requires a $100,000 withdrawal from their account. The chart uses today's tax bracket (2020) and no standard deduction was used. As you can see, not all of the $100,000 is taxed at the same rate. The chart shows that withdrawing from a taxable account will cause a higher tax rate. The maximum rate taxed in this example is 22%.

Results with a Combination of Taxable and Non-tax Accounts (Figure 4.3)

Taxable Income		Taxable Income	Plus	Non-Tax
Pension, 401k, 403b, IRA		Pension, 401k, 403b, IRA		Roth/IUL
$100,000 (withdrawal)		$50,000 (withdrawal)		$ 50,000
($0-$19750) x 10%	$ 1,975	($0-$19,750) x 10%	$1,975	
($80,250 - $19,750) x 12%	$ 7,260	($50,000 - $19,750) x 12%	$4,345	
($100,000 - $80,250) x 22%	$ 4,345	$50,000 - $5,605 Total Tax	$5,605	
$100,000 - $13,580 Total Tax	$ 13,580	$44,395 +		$ 50,000
$ 86,420		$ 94,395		

However, when you have a combination of taxable and non-taxable income, you reduce the tax rate from 22% to 12%. This example shows that even if taxes stay at the same rate, a non-taxable account like a Roth or an IUL will be a tremendous asset and will help you lower taxes in the future.

Get your tax bill settled now while taxes are still low, rather than waiting until later when your taxes will be much higher.

What is a Roth IRA?

Option 2 is a Roth IRA. Unlike a traditional IRA, a Roth IRA uses after-tax dollars. Roth is an individual retirement account that is not taxed upon distribution. Qualified withdrawals from the Roth IRA plan are tax-free, and the growth in the account is also tax-free. There are no age limits with a Roth IRA as long as you claim income.

There are also no minimum required distributions at 72, so you have complete flexibility with how and when you withdraw your money during retirement. Even better, since Roth IRA distributions don't add to your annual income, a Roth could reduce the possibility of having to pay tax on Social Security benefits, or premium surcharges for Medicare Part B and Part D.

These are just a few reasons why Roth IRAs are so popular. Roth IRAs are recommended by advisors and conversions are attractive for individuals who want to reduce their tax liability when they are in retirement. Also, Roth IRAs appeal to older and wealthier people who want their heirs to inherit a legacy that's tax-free.

Roth IRAs are considered a poor man's account because it has limits on how much a person can invest annually. A high-income earner who wants to contribute a large sum of money into a tax-free retirement account can't use only Roth IRAs. For them, IULs should be utilized.

A legal way a high-income earner can work around the Roth's income limits is with a strategy called the backdoor Roth IRA. Presently, like a traditional IRA, annual income limits are $6,000 per year per person (if you're under age 50) or $7,000 (if you're above age 50) per year. A person can open both traditional IRAs and Roth IRAs for themselves, wife and kids. The way this strategy works is to put money in a traditional IRA and then convert the account to a Roth IRA to avoid taxes in the future.

Roth Conversions

With a Roth conversion, investors are able to transfer money out of a traditional IRA, pay taxes on the funds at ordinary federal and state rates, and then move the money into the Roth. Once the money is in the Roth, it will grow tax-free. To avoid a 10% penalty after converting the account, the money must remain in the Roth IRA for five years before taking a tax-free distribution. If you're at least age 59 1/2 when you make the withdrawal, you won't pay the 10% early withdrawal even if it's a conversion.

There are presently no limits on the number of Roth conversions or on the dollar amounts you may convert. If you wish, you can convert from multiple accounts and you are also permitted to convert a traditional IRA at any age. The converted balance will be calculated as part of your annual income and taxed appropriately. Once the transfer is complete and the funds are deposited into your new Roth IRA, you are free to invest the funds for tax-free growth.

Roth conversions are very popular and many people are taking advantage of the current low tax rate, choosing to pay taxes on their funds now. Even with all the benefits, a Roth conversion is still a major decision. Some of the factors to consider are the current income tax rate, your anticipated income tax rate in the future, the new Secure Act changes, and your need for long term care benefits. It's also important to make sure you can afford to pay the taxes the conversion will create.

Roth IRAs have many uses and are a very popular choice when it comes to tax-free accounts. But the number one choice for a tax-free investment vehicle is the Index Universal Life Insurance (IUL). In most cases, anything that a Roth IRA can do, an IUL could do better.

Summary

The lessons learned in this chapter are:

1. 401(k)s and Pensions are the best retirement accounts because they provide Free Money.
2. Stop contributing to IRAs and 403(b)s; instead, open after-tax accounts.
3. A combination of taxable and nontaxable accounts will reduce taxes.
4. Roth conversions is a strategy used to reduce taxes in the future.

Chapter 5
IULs: Your Best Choice for More Tax-Free Income?

Let's say it was time for you to take a vacation and you decided to go to Las Vegas because you wanted to see some of the shows and you also wanted to gamble. When you arrived at your hotel, you found out there were two types of casinos in town.

The first casino is like every other casino. You can go there, have fun, gamble your money, and if you win, you get to keep all the money. But, if you lose, you pay for all your losses.

The second casino is different. If you gamble and win, you can take home your winnings up to a defined limit. And if you lose, you can still go home with the same amount of money that you came with. You won't lose even one dollar! The great thing about this is that you can visit this casino every day and all your winnings get credited to your account. Those winnings are locked into your account forever. You can't ever lose any of the money you came with...and you can't ever lose any of the money you won before!

At which casino would you prefer to play, the first casino or the second casino?

Obviously the second casino is the smart choice. It's not even considered gambling when you can't lose. If the second casino actually existed, there would be huge lines of people waiting to get in, and why not? Why would anyone want to go to the other casinos?

This is exactly how an Indexed Universal Life (IUL) insurance policy works. This is the only investment that is IRS-approved where your money can earn the returns of a stock market index, lock-in all of your annual gains, and never lose a dime when the market has a negative annual performance. On top of that, any withdrawals you make are all tax-free. Without a doubt, this is a one-of-a-kind retirement investment opportunity.

Remember the words of the immortal Warren Buffett:

Rule #1: Never lose money.

Rule #2: Never forget Rule #1.

With an Indexed Universal Life insurance policy, you will never lose your money, and the money your account earns each year is added to your next year's balance and also can never be taken from you. Your account never suffers a loss.

Take a look at the chart below. It shows the growth of an account over a five-year period during the time of the Great Recession in 2008. One of the lines is an IUL account, and the other line shows a stock market index account.

Comparison of an IUL Account with a Stock Market Account (Figure 5.1)

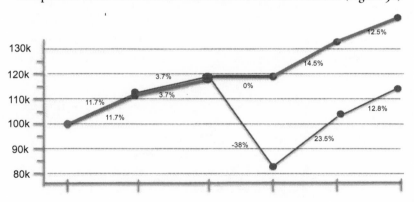

What you'll notice is that in the first two years, both accounts performed at the same rate, and both accounts were each worth $120,000. Then, just after 2007, the two accounts separated. The stock market account fell heavily, losing about $40,000 in value, winding up somewhere just above $80,000. But notice that the IUL account lost 0% and kept its wealth at about $120,000 of value. While there was no growth that year, neither was there any loss. Not a penny.

Then, as 2008 continued, both accounts increased in value, but even though the stock market index account gained about 35% in two years, from 2008 to 2010, it was unable to duplicate the performance of the IUL account. That's because it takes time to regain losses, but if you don't ever have losses, the wealth in your account can grow without interruption.

When an account loses -20% for example, the account goes to 80%. Now it takes 25%, not 20%, of that 80% to return to its original value. As you can see from the illustration, it's hard to catch-up once you lose money, so the message here is to never lose money. That's what Warren Buffett said, and that's what your Indexed Universal Life insurance policy was created to do.

With a whole life insurance policy, the premiums allow you to build the cash value of the policy so you can provide a larger death benefit for your heirs when you die, and the funds are not available to you while you are still living.

An IUL is different because the objective is to satisfy the smallest death benefit requirement and pay out the maximum premium allowed. The more money that's deposited in your policy, the faster the investment portion of your policy will grow as your money compounds.

In addition, the IUL is also the most flexible permanent insurance on the market. As the cash value increases, there will come a point where the cash value could be used to pay your policy's premiums, or even stop paying the premiums completely. As mentioned before, you can borrow against your policy through a policy loan, and you can choose whether or not to ever pay these loans back. In essence, you are borrowing from yourself.

The average net annual rate of return for an IUL is between 6% - 9%, and as you know now, your investment is completely safe from all risks when the market goes down. Since the premiums you are paying are made with after-tax money, all withdrawals and all loans are always tax-free, and there is no required IRS reporting.

Let's look at the next illustration which shows the IUL account of a 30-year-old male named Tony who started his account by depositing $1,000 per month in after-tax dollars. The average rate of return is a conservative 6.7% with the growth of the policy capped at 10.3% in the S&P 500 Index.

You can see that in the very first year, Tony has contributed $12,000 at

IUL Account with 6.27% Average Annual Increase (Figure 5.2)

			Illustrated With Index Credits: 6,27%			
Year	Age	Premium	Total Dist.	Account Value	Surrender Value	Death Benefit
1*+	30/31	12,000.00	0	8,743	0	$927.349
10	39/40	12,000.00	0	116,975	116,975	$1.035.349
		12,000.00	0			
30	59/60	12,000.00	0	997,465	997,465	$1.336.603
		360,000.00	0			
31	60/61	0.00	111,816	1,074,554	959,571	$1.281.937
40	69/70	0.00	111,816	2,052,400	587,804	$916.187
		360,000.00	1,118,160			
50	79/80	0.00	111,816	2,236,320	213,139	$419.412
		360,000.00	2,236,320			
59	88/89	0.00	111,816	7,607,454	114,217	$494.589
60	89/90	0.00	111,816	3,354,480	125,834	$532.281
		360,000.00	3,354,480			
61	90/91	0.00	111,816	8,682,771	142,916	$577.054
70	99/100	0.00	0	16,228,947	2,671,100	$2.671.100
		360,000.00	3,466,296			

$1,000 per month; on the first day of his policy Tony has a death benefit of $927,349. Every year the death benefit increases, so should something tragic happen, Tony's heirs are taken care of for life.

After 10 years of contributions, the account value is $116,975, almost equal to Tony's total deposits. But then, with Year 11, the cash value is making enough interest to pay for the cost of insurance, and the premiums Tony continues to contribute are going directly into the cash value of his account.

After 30 years, Tony has a cash value of $997,465, almost three times the amount of the premiums he's paid.

When Tony is 61, in Year 31, he is no longer making monthly contributions. Instead, even before he is eligible for Social Security, Tony can start receiving loans from his policy of $111,816 every year until he is 90 years old...and all of it is tax-free.

Tony's total contributions are $360,000 and after 10 years, the total annual withdrawals equal $1,118,160. After 20 years Tony has withdrawn a total $2,236,320 and after 30 years his withdrawals grow to $3,354,480. All of this money is tax-free. Also, there is still a death benefit for Tony's heirs of $532,281 which continues to grow.

Now you can see the power of Indexed Universal Life insurance. There is no other asset with which you can potentially earn this amount of net returns...with no risk...and have access to tax-free income for the rest of your life while leaving a healthy death benefit to your heirs, also tax-free.

This is an unbelievable investment!

The next illustration shows the returns for two very popular allocations made in the S&P 500 Index over a 12-year period. In the first column, labeled "Annual PTP" (annual point to point), you can see that the S&P 500 Index had a -38.5% loss in 2008 during the Great Recession, but the IUL had a loss of 0% because the policy's floor protected the policy owner. As you look at the chart, you can see that the annual cap of 10.3% for this IUL policy was reached eight times during this 12-year span.

S&P 500 Index Performance Comparison (Figure 5.3)

End Year	S & P 500 Annual PTP		S & P 500 Annual PTP w/Spread	
	Index Change	Return for Index Selection	Index Change	Return for Index Selection
2008	-38.5%	0.0%	-38.5%	0.0%
2009	23.5%	10.3%	23.5%	17.3%
2010	12.8%	10.3%	12.8%	6.3%
2011	1.5%	1.5%	1.5%	0.0%
2012	13.4%	10.3%	13.4%	6.9%
2013	29.6%	10.3%	29.6%	23.1%
2014	11.4%	10.3%	11.4%	4.9%
2015	-0.7%	0.0%	-0.7%	0.0%
2016	10.5%	10.3%	10.5%	4.0%
2017	20.4%	10.3%	20.4%	13.9%
2018	-6.2%	0.0%	-6.2%	0.0%
2019	28.9%	10.3%	28.9%	22.4%

Spread 6.5%
29.6% - 6.5% = 23.1%

The chart above shows the comparison between two investment choices. The first option has a return capped at 10.3%. The second option has no cap, but it does have a 6.5% "Spread" or fee.

Take a look at Year 2013. The S&P 500 Index return was 29.6%. In the first column, the account was credited 10.3%, which is the high-end cap for this policy. In the second column, the allocation was 29.6% minus the spread of 6.5%, so the account was credited 23.1%.

Can you imagine earning a 23.1% return in one year with a fixed product? These kinds of returns are possible with this company. When the market returns more than 16.8% (10.3 cap + 6.5 margin), the account with the margin will be the better option. High returns are possible with IULs but our illustrations are created with a conservative 6.27%. The cap of 6.67% and the margin of 6.5% go up or down every year, and they are not guaranteed for the life of the policy.

As you already know, you can place different allocations in different index funds as long as the total equals 100%. You can adjust these allocations as you wish every year during your anniversary month.

When you overfund your IUL, the combination of extra contributions and compound interest can potentially generate enormous amounts of nontaxable cash value in your policy. This cash value is available to fund your tax-free retirement.

Of course, the sooner you get started and the longer you wait to access your money, the larger your cash value will grow. Time is an important factor.

Another benefit of having an IUL is that if you need to, you can have access to the death benefit while you're still alive if you suffer from what's called "Critical, Chronic, or Terminal Illness".

So, not only are you building an incredible tax-free retirement lifestyle, but you also have access to the funds when you get sick. This beats the pants off 401(k)s, IRAs, and any pension plan.

Warning!

While many insurance companies offer Indexed Universal Life insurance, not all IULs are created equally. Only a few IUL policies will earn the high returns you saw illustrated in this chapter. We can recommend those to you when we meet.

Remember, too, that some insurance agents do a better job for you than others. Many agents design IUL policies that benefit the company and benefit themselves rather than their client. It's also true that not all agents really understand what they're doing. Some are only doing what they are told to do, and others are greedy, trying to line their own pockets at your expense.

There are a number of factors you have to check in choosing an insurance company for your IUL. Look for the company's rating, caps, living benefits, and cost of insurance. Remember that just because an insurance company has a good rating or is well-known does not mean their IUL is any good. There are too many important factors to explain in one chapter, but we would be happy to meet with you and go over this information in detail.

However, here is something I can explain. The illustration above (5.2) shows two options. One is Option A (level) and the other is Option B (increasing). You can see that the death benefit increases from $927k to $1.2 million. That is Option B (increasing). This option is best for the client, but the commission for the agent decreases around 50%.

The main reason why many greedy insurance agents pick Option A is because it pays the highest commission. Option A is good for an older individual and is not good for a younger person whose main purpose is to grow the cash value and death benefit.

Many companies offer higher commissions or big bonuses to sell their products, which means that the product is good for the company but not always the best choice for the client.

Take a Loan from Your Own IUL

Let's refer again to Tony's chart above. As Tony begins annual distributions at age 61, he is borrowing $111,816 every year in distributions as a loan from his IUL. The loan rate varies, but in this case it was 4%. This is a great loan to have because Tony's IUL continues to earn an average of 6.27%, and his loan rate is 4%. His IUL is earning +2.27% more than he's paying!

When a person has a loan in which they are paying less than what they are making, that is an example of a good loan. Loans like this one should never be paid back. Many other companies design their IULs to use a fixed rate, so they charge the same rate as the rate they credit your account. In the business it's known as having a net zero or "wash" rate.

In the chart below, you can see that a fixed rate results in a $0 net gain for the policyholder, but a variable rate results in additional money that can be used for retirement or for the death benefit. Many companies do not offer this special feature, but we know the few that do.

Example of $100,000 Loan
with 4% Variable Rate and 6.27% Return (Figure 5.4)

Loan Type	Fixed	Variable
Interest Cost	4%	$ 4,000
Gain (On Loan)	4%	$ 6,270
Net Gain	**0%**	**$ 2,270**

Fees

Something else you have to watch out for are the fees. As you can see with Tony's example, his first two years have a cash value of $0. This is because the fees are always higher at the beginning. There is a cost for setting up the policy and the commission must be paid. However, when the IUL is properly designed with a minimum death benefit and maximized premiums, the fees are much smaller.

The longer you keep the insurance policy, the cheaper the fees become. By the time you reach life expectancy, the fees are only about 0.5% per year. Other retirement plans like whole life, 401(k)s, and 403(b)s have much higher fees that typically range from 2% - 4%.

Comparing IULs with Other Types of Permanent Life Insurance

Whole life: Whole life insurance returns an average of around 3% per year. Whole life insurance will give the policyholder dividends but growth is slow. Whole life responds well in good market conditions but can barely keep up with inflation.

Universal Life Insurance: Universal Life Insurance (UL) usually returns between 2% - 5%, but generally averages less than 4%. ULs have lower returns and growth is based on a flat dividend rate established by the company's assumptions. This means that the insurance company decides every year how much money will be credited to your account. The older the policy, the higher the fees your account must pay, and usually the insurance company will increase the premiums to prevent the policy from lapsing.

Variable Universal Life: Variable Universal Life insurance (VUL) has a cash value component that allows investment in sub-accounts within the policy. These sub-accounts are pinned to the performance of mutual funds. While you have complete control over which sub-accounts your money will be invested, these accounts have the potential to lose a lot of money, as much as 30% - 40% just as they did in 2008 and 2020. It's a real gamble when you put your money into a VUL because the loss of your account's value is not a matter of if, but when.

The Results You Want

I have spent a great deal of time comparing a wide variety of retirement investment plans and companies, and I have found there are only two IUL companies that rise to the top. It just doesn't matter what your specifics are, whether the policy is for a newborn, a 30-year-old, or 60-year-old. These two companies are consistently the best two companies from which to buy your IUL. These two companies offer IULs that are better than any other permanent life insurance, Roth IRA, 401(k) or 401(b). If you want reliable growth that can put you in the retirement lifestyle you want, these are the only two companies to consider.

You may have heard that Albert Einstein, the most brilliant man we know, once said that compound interest is the most powerful force in the entire universe. Here is his actual quote: "Compound interest is the 8th wonder of the world. He who understands it, earns it; he who doesn't, pays it."

If Einstein was alive today, he would probably say that IULs are the greatest invention man ever created for building wealth. That's because IULs connect very well with the Rule of 72, which is a useful formula for calculating the annual compounded return of an investment.

A well-designed IUL could solve most people's money problems and provide funds for your children's college expenses, your mortgage, emergencies, a hefty death benefit for your heirs, a safe and secure retirement lifestyle, and even benefits like long-term care.

We're not talking about being a genius to do this. In fact, it's easy. The sooner you start an IUL for yourself, for your children, and for your grandchildren, the more spectacular the results will be. It does not matter how old you are, and it does not matter how much money you have. Get started right away because an IUL can be a tremendous help, the solution you've been looking for.

Of course you need to find an honest and knowledgeable insurance agent who puts your financial needs ahead of his or her commissions, an agent who is familiar with the top companies offering IULs. The agent you select will help you design a policy that meets your needs within your budget.

Now that you have seen the charts and have read the comparisons with other products, it's clear that IULs are the best retirement vehicle ever created. IULs have been called "the new 403(b) and IRA". This book was written to show you why you should stop investing in 401(k)s, 403(b)s, and IRAs. It's time for you to change the way you think and invest so you can maximize your time by investing in an Indexed Life Insurance policy that will create the wealth you desire.

Summary

The lessons learned in this chapter are:

1. Create an IUL with a minimum death benefit and larger deposits to the cash value account.
2. The younger you start, the more time your IUL has to grow.
3. An IUL lets you access your own death benefit if necessary, unlike 401(k)s, 403(b)s, and IRAs.
4. Not all IULs are created equally, and not all agents are honest.
5. Variable loans on IULs should be utilized and they are a powerful tool.
6. IULs are the best investment ever created and are better investments than 401(k)s, 403(b)s, and both IRAs.

Chapter 6
Comparing the IUL with the Roth IRA

What is the best option... a Roth IRA or an IUL? We now have an opportunity to learn about both as after-tax investment products suitable for your retirement funding.

Taxes are one of our biggest concerns, a huge issue that most people are dealing with today and which need to be dealt with by your heirs after your death. No one knows how much we will be paying for our taxes in the future. We do know that taxes right now are at one of the lowest rates in history, that these favorable tax rates will not last forever, and that our powerful country is deep in debt. Everyone knows this situation is going to get much worse before we and our children have to start paying for these disturbing circumstances.

What is the best solution for taxpayers today? Pay your taxes now when taxes are low, stop contributing to deferred-tax accounts, and start tax-free accounts like a Roth IRA or Index Universal Life Insurance (IUL) immediately.

The Roth IRA and Indexed Universal Life (IUL) policies are products which have already been taxed, and your withdrawals are tax-free. These financial tools are excellent even if you believe taxes will be the same in the future.

Investors have different financial circumstances and needs, so determining which product is best for you depends on your personal situation. The chart below compares both products, showing their differences.

In this chart you can clearly compare the major differences. An IUL includes a death benefit on Day One. That means the person has to be insurable and have average health. The IUL is a rich man's account because there is no annual $6,000 limit.

Differences Between an IUL and a Roth IRA (Figure 6.1)

Option 1: Index Universal Life		Option 2: Roth IRA
I. U. L.		*ROTH*
Market Protection	⟷	NO Market Protection
Tax-Free Benefit		Tax-Free Benefit
Benefits on Day 1	⟷	NO Benefits on Day 1
NO Pre-Payment on Loans		NO Loans
RICH Man Account	⟷	POOR Man Account
Supports "Own Banker" Concept		NO "Own Banker" Concept
No Early Withdrawal Penalty	⟷	Early Withdrawal Penalty
Accessible Tax-Free At Any time		Accessible Tax-Free After Age 59 1/2
NO Minimum Distribution at Age 72	⟷	NO Minimum Distribution at Age 72
Can NOT Be Altered By Changes in Law		Can Be Altered By Changes in Law
Conversion From Taxable Account	⟷	Conversion From Taxable Account
Earnings NOT Included in Income		Earnings NOT Included in Income

The IUL is also perfect for a new-born because no income is needed. With an IUL, money can be withdrawn tax-free at any time. One feature the chart does not show that is very important is how loans work inside an IUL policy. With a Roth, you don't have loans and you must make withdrawals if you want to access your cash. In an IUL, the loan amounts are still held in the policy's cash value. Earnings are still being credited into your account, minus the cost of the loan fee. These IUL loans were explained in the previous chapter.

To better understand, let's look at the next illustration comparing both accounts using the same rate of return and same distribution amounts. In this illustration, a 30-year-old is contributing the maximum annual amount for a Roth IRA, which is $6,000 per year. The IRS strictly caps the amount of contributions to a Roth IRA each year, so accumulating wealth with this product is difficult compared with an IUL where

Roth IRA and an IUL for a 25-year old (Figure 6.2)

			Roth IRA/Non Taxable		Index Universal Life (IUL)		
			1 Cash Withdrawal	2 Account Value	1 Cash Withdrawal	2 Account Value	3 Death Benefit
Yr	Age	Deposit					
1	25	6,000	0	6,300	0	0	405,145
2	26	6,000	0	12,915	0	3,211	410,621
20	44	6,000	0	208,316	0	210,520	610,52
30	54	6,000	0	418,565	0	501,638	901,638
34	58	6,000	0	535,922	0	685,162	1,085,162
35	59	6,000	0	569,018	0	739,258	1,139,258
36	60	0	68,897	525,127	68,897	718,068	1,118,068
46	70	0	16,962	0	68,897	498,495	898,495
47	71	0	0	0	68,897	477,356	877,356
65	89	0	0	0	68,897	360,171	760,171
66	90	0	0	0	68,897	381,495	781,495
67	91	0	0	0	0	479,482	879,482
68	92	0	0	0	0	584,716	984,716
		210,000	705,932		2,135,807		

accumulation happens much faster.

The interest rate of 6.27% was used in this illustration for both products. As you can see, the Roth IRA starts out strong but the IUL catches up quickly. After 30 years, the annual contributions of $6,000 stop and distributions of $68,897 per year begin for both products. Now, at this point, the Roth has $569,018 and the IUL has $739,258. The fees on IULs are less and it also pays dividends and bonuses. The Roth has deposits of $210,000 and distributions of $705,932 before it runs out of money. The Roth looks very good until you compare it with the IUL. The IUL's total distributions are $2,135,807 at age 90, about 300% more! Also, the death benefit is still $984,716 at age 92 and it continues to multiply. This is the incredible power of an IUL.

If you only plan to invest 20 years or less and then withdraw all the money, it might not matter which product you pick. If you are interested in the best product for retirement income, you should start an IUL as soon as possible. It does not matter if you start an IUL with $100 a month or $10,000 a month because given enough time, the IUL beats every other investment product. The younger you are, the more time you have to compound your investment, and the greater the chance you are in good health and insurable.

Roth Conversions

In the previous chapter we talked about Roth conversions. We can convert funds from a taxable account like a 403(b), 401(k) or a traditional IRA into a Roth IRA. Taxes are paid according to your current tax rate and the tax penalty of 10% is waived. This can be done at any age and for any dollar amount. The $6,000 annual Roth IRA limit does not apply here.

Conversion to an IUL is best when the person is older than 59 ½ in order to avoid the 10% penalty. In the next illustration, a 60-year-old has contributed $100,000 per year for 10 years into both an IUL and a Roth IRA. The interest rate used in this illustration is a conservative 6.27%.

Conversion of a Roth IRA and an IUL (Figure 6.3)

Yr	Age	Deposit	Roth IRA		Index Universal Life (IUL)		
			1 Cash Withdrawal	2 Account Value	1 Cash Withdrawal	2 Account Value	3 Death Benefit
1	60	100,000	0	100,999	0	12,284	1,762,003
2	61	100,000	0	207,257	0	109,945	1,862,003
10	69	100,000	0	1,282,711	0	1,097,686	2,662,003
11	70	0	92,440	1,252,252	92,440	1,075,598	2,564,516
32	91	0	92,440	80,687	92,440	361,564	534,619
33	92	0	80,687	0	92,440	349,568	488,418
41	100	0	0	0	92,440	585,006	585,006
42	101	0	0	0	0	764,385	764,385

Immediately on approval of the policy, he has a death benefit of $1,762,003. Then, after contributing $100,000 per year for 10 years, the cash value is $1,097,686. The beauty of this policy begins as soon as distributions start at age 70. At this point, the cash value never depletes. Annual distributions are $92,440 per year for the next 30 years up to age 100...with a total distribution of $2,773,200...250% of the total contributions made between ages 60 – 69. The cash value and the death benefit continue to grow.

Compare these results with the Roth IRA. It had total distributions of $1,837,047 ($92,440 x 19 + $80,687) and ran out of money by age 92. Clearly, there is NO comparison.

If the individual is younger than 59 ½, a Roth conversion is recommended. These conversions could either be into a variable interest rate product or a fixed rate product. For fixed Index-based products, see Figure 11.1.

Indexed Universal Life insurance is considered the new IRA, and 403(b). An IUL is a good fit for someone at any age who is in good health because it has so many uses. The younger a person starts an IUL, the more incredible the results will be, and the more likely the person is insurable (in good health). Find out what fits your needs, whether a Roth IRA or an IUL. Contact us for a free IUL illustration that will clearly show the potential financial benefits available for you and your loved ones when you start now.

A person should always consider all their options and seek professional advice from an independent agent. Remember, NOT all companies offering IULs are created equally, and NOT all agents are properly trained to really understand the true value of an IUL. My company specializes in IULs and we can help you find the perfect investment to safeguard your financial future.

Hopefully this chapter has explained the differences between a Roth IRA and an IUL, and why one may work better for you than another.

Summary

The lessons learned in this chapter are:

1. Roth IRAs and IULs are two great products with different uses.
2. Compare the advantages of both products before making a decision.
3. Illustrations specifically for you and your unique circumstances are available and free for the asking.

Chapter 7
Designing Your IUL for Maximum Performance

All my clients are unique and have different financial needs. Most of these needs can be resolved when an IUL is designed properly because an IUL is the best financial vehicle in the marketplace today. A properly designed IUL can provide you with a maximum tax-free death benefit, the massive accumulation of tax-deferred income, and the availability of tax-free loans you can access through the account.

When designing your IUL, I meet with you to understand your financial goals and review the elements of your financial situation. As mentioned earlier in this book, different companies offer different IULs, and not every IUL is designed to deliver the benefits you would otherwise enjoy unless you have an experienced adviser to guide you.

Many companies have well-known names and strong ratings, but this does not mean they provide good IULs. Also, few agents or advisers truly understand how to structure an IUL, and many are selling their company's products because of the high commissions and high bonuses they receive. These agents aren't always motivated or sufficiently trained to ensure you receive the maximum benefits and return on your investment. You must be very careful when purchasing an IUL because not all agents are the same, and not all insurance companies offer the best IULs available.

I have spent years analyzing and working with Indexed Universal Life (IUL) products, teaching my clients about their value and guiding my clients toward making the best selection for their unique financial circumstances. There are many different factors to consider including the different contract variables, pricing models and costs, legalities, and arranging the best possible outcomes for all my clients.

Also, there are many important details that must be done correctly when structuring an IUL so it delivers a healthy death and living benefit that maximizes your rate of return and ensures your financial success. Planning for retirement requires careful thought, expert industry knowledge, years of experience, and a commitment to providing the best service for you.

Here are some recommendations I advise my clients to consider, and please remember to also refer to the illustrations in Chapter 5, "IULs: Your Best Choice for More Income".

Rule #1: Maximize the cash value. Most IULs are designed to maximize the cash value of the policy so the cash value can provide the regular monthly income for living expenses a retiree needs for the remainder of his or her life. Compared with a whole life insurance policy, the Indexed Universal Life policy is a much better value.

Rule #2: Buy the smallest death benefit possible. You want to buy a policy that gives you the smallest amount of death benefit for the highest premium. Fees for the policy are based on the death benefit amount that you purchase, with the left-over premium amount deposited in the cash value portion of your policy. This way you can keep your policy costs down while also maximizing the amount of money going into your indexed investment account.

The smaller the death benefit, the lower your fees. The lower your fees, the more money will be deposited into your policy's cash value. The more money you have in your cash value, the faster your cash value and the interest it's earning will compound. The faster this money increases through growth and compounding, the more tax-free cash is available to you either during your accumulation period, or when you need the money for retirement income during your distribution period.

When an IUL is designed properly, there will also be a substantial death benefit for your heirs.

Rule #3: Buy the "Increasing Option" death benefit if you are under 50. When you purchase your IUL and you are under 50 years old, it's important that your policy is designed with an "increasing" death benefit, not a "leveled" death benefit. With an increasing death benefit option, the death benefit will increase as the cash value starts accumulating and accelerating. It's important to note that the increasing option is in the best interests of the client, but not the agent. The agent's commission decreases by more than half with an increasing option, so most agents will steer you toward a leveled death benefit so their commission will be higher. However, if you are over 50 years old, the leveled option is recommended because this will keep the cost of your insurance lower.

Rule #4: Take loans, not withdrawals. One of the advantageous features of the IUL is that you can access your money by taking out loans against the cash value in your policy. A well-designed IUL should allow you to take distributions as variable loans against the cash value.

By taking a variable loan against your cash value, the amount of money you are borrowing against your policy continues to yield interest even though the money is not in your account. This interest is credited to the cash value in your account and you are earning interest on money that's not there. Of course, you have to find the right company because not every insurance company allows this.

Rule #5: Start as early as possible. You've heard this many times before. The sooner you start, the more time there is for the cash value in your investment account to multiply. Not only do you have more time to increase your wealth, but the cost of the insurance is much less and this makes the monthly premiums less as well.

Usually young people have lots of investment time but very little capital to invest. It's possible to design their policy so the contributions increase in later years when they are more financially capable of making larger premium payments.

Something to keep in mind is that it's possible to maximize the allowable amount of your policy early, and if this happens you will need to apply for a larger death benefit. This means going through underwriting again. However, when your agent or adviser is experienced and understands the best way to design your policy, he can make sure the policy has room for increasing the young person's future contributions so your policy will meet all their financial needs and goals without having to go through underwriting a second time.

The older you are, the higher the cost of insurance and the less time you have for the cash value to multiply. Higher deposits will be required and an experienced agent can help design a policy to meet your objective.

Rule #6: Buy more than one IUL. If you should reach the maximum limits of your first IUL, you should apply for a second IUL so you can keep expanding the benefits of this excellent tax-free income vehicle. You should also consider opening an IUL for your spouse, and also for your children as soon as possible. You can keep ownership of these accounts and control all the decisions while also securing income and the many other IUL benefits for your spouse and children.

Rule #7: Don't allow your IUL policy to become an endowment contract. In an IUL, there are minimum and maximum payments allowed. Overfunding the policy is recommended to a certain limit. When payment exceeds the amount allowed, it becomes a Modified Endowment Contract.

When this happens, your withdrawals will be taxed as ordinary income instead of tax-free income.

Since the main purpose of having an IUL is to build tax-free wealth and take tax-free withdrawals, having your IUL policy convert into a modified endowment contract is counterproductive.

Rule #8: Consider a hybrid policy. If your current financial position makes it too difficult for you to afford the premiums for an IUL but you believe you will be able to pay them in the future, consider buying a term insurance policy that has a convertible option into an IUL. I have been helping people do this for years and have designed many combinations of IULs with term insurance policies. There is a big advantage to this strategy because you will immediately possess a higher death benefit while also having a stable retirement income later.

Rule #9: Buy an IUL for your children and grandchildren. You can also secure the financial future of your children and grandchildren by getting them started with their own IUL as soon as possible. Imagine giving a legacy like this to the young people in your family. The cost of insurance is low for them so you'll only need to make minimum payments. Because your children and grandchildren are young, they have decades of time for the cash value to multiply. If they wish, when they get older and have careers, they could increase their premiums and the death benefit to meet all their retirement needs, thanks to you.

Now that you've had a chance to understand the value of having an IUL for yourself and your family, and you've studied the illustrations and read the comparisons of IULs with other investment products, you can now see that IULs are the best retirement vehicle ever created.

It's also clear that when you overfund these IULs, you can potentially generate huge amounts of nontaxable cash value in your policy, all of it growing tax-free and available to you as tax-free income when you are in your distribution phase.

The IUL is the most flexible permanent insurance product on the market and can be a highly valuable asset to your investment portfolio when it is correctly structured.

Remember, it's critical that you work with an agent or adviser who has years of experience, understands the IUL investment inside and out, and has your best financial interests in mind. Also remember that there are many companies offering IULs but only a few offer high quality IUL products. Knowing which companies have the best IUL products requires a great deal of analysis and study, which is a specialty I am pleased to offer you.

Summary

The lessons learned in this chapter are:

1. A properly designed IUL is customized for each client because every client has their own unique financial circumstances.
2. An IUL is designed to maximize cash value so the cash value can be used as a source of tax-free income while you are still alive.

3. Purchase your IUL as soon as you can because the more time you have, the more your cash value can multiply. The cost of your insurance is cheaper the younger you are, so the premiums are smaller.

4. You can purchase an IUL for your spouse and children while being the owner of the account and controlling all decisions.

5. If the IUL premiums are too high for you now, consider buying a term insurance policy that has an option allowing you to convert the term policy into an IUL later.

Chapter 8
Texas Teachers: You Must Know This!

As you probably know, I am a former Texas high school mathematics teacher with 20 years of experience. I have taught every level of mathematics from fundamentals to pre-calculus, and because of my experience as an educator in the Texas public school system, I know a lot about TRS (Teacher Retirement System) because my own retirement funds were once held there. Here is very important information that every educator should know.

Let's begin by understanding how the current TRS system is failing Texas teachers. In a nutshell, here are four of the most disappointing aspects of the TRS program:

1. TRS is a bad Pension plan and it is getting worse.
2. TRS has one of the worst investment vehicles in a 403(b).
3. TRS has a bad supplemental insurance purchasing system.
4. TRS has the most expensive Medicare Advantage Plan in the state.

Sorry, most public-school educators love the TRS system and are loyal to TRS. TRS is the only system they have known and believe that TRS will take care of them. Most teachers don't know some very disturbing details about TRS, and they haven't taken the opportunity to compare the TRS retirement program with other pensions.

Let me keep this simple. If you were hired after 2007, please pay close attention.

TRS provides a defined benefit plan, which means it is a pension plan. Your pension is determined by a preset formula based on your salary and years of service, not the amount of funds accumulated in your account. In other words, your pension payout will not be based on your individual contributions to the retirement system or the interest it has created. It is based only on your age and years of service.

Here is an illustration to help you understand the mathematics:

Calculating Your TRS Annuity (Figure 8.1)

CALCULATING YOUR ANNUITY					
Highest annual salaries:	2019-20	2018-19	2017-18	2016-17	2015-16
	$ 63,980	$ 65,507	$ 63,980	$ 59,074	$ 61,507
Highest average salary:	$ 62,808				
Years of service credit:	33				
Total service	33 x 2.300 = 75.90%				
	$62 x 75.90 = $47,671 Standard Annuity per year (gross)				
	$47,671 / 12 = $3,972.61 Standard Annuity per month (gross)				

This is a hypothetical example of a teacher named Joanne. She is 55 years old and had 33 years of experience teaching in the state of Texas. Joanne's years of experience are multiplied by 2.3%, which is the percentage of her full pension that she will receive (33 yrs x 2.3 = 75.9%) That percentage is multiplied by her five-year average salary and that determines her yearly gross pension. In this case $62,808 x 75.9% = $47,671.

Joanne will receive 75.9%, and this is a 24.1% loss in income, which is a very severe amount of money to lose. This is known as the Gap, and most teachers are not aware they should be paying attention to this. The Gap is the percentage of income teachers lose when compared to the actual salary they will have when they retire. To cover the Gap, teachers should consider opening personal retirement accounts. Remember what we learned in Chapter 5, that a 403(b) is not a good idea.

An employee is eligible to receive their pension payouts when the sum of their age and years of service total 80. For example, a teacher with 20 service years must be at least 60 years old in order to receive what is called a full retirement.

Other state employees have pension plans that don't use age nor years of service to determine a pension amount.

When employees are ready to retire, the money in their account is annuitized into monthly payments. These state pensions don't have penalties like TRS if one decides to retire early. These plans are serving thousands of employees in the Texas public sector today.

These two plans are the Texas Municipal Retirement System (TMRS) and the Texas County and District Retirement System (TCDRS).

These plans have much more flexibility than TRS. Cities and counties make decisions on the contributions, matching funds if any, and guarantee a specific rate of return. Members of these plans can retire early and get a pension that is based on the accumulation of their investments, not years of service

TRS and Texas could choose to adopt these plans for school districts and teachers to replace the failing system. However, as of today, TRS has no plans to improve or change the coming apocalypse, and no plans for enrolling employees in Social Security.

TRS is Going Broke

Most people believe that a pension is good for workers, but this is not always the case. Texas legislators have created a pension plan that is notably stingy, favoring the employer and not the employee. Texas teachers are required to contribute 7.7% of their salary (2019) and the state of Texas will match that contribution. That might appear quite generous, but 5.34% of this money is allocated for the payment of unfunded state liabilities, not to fund teacher retirement benefits. This means that Texas employers are only contributing about 2.36% toward teacher retirement benefits. You might be surprised to realize that this is less than a typical 401(k) provides, and less than the teacher retirement plans of many other states.

The bottom line is that most of an employer's contributions are being used to pay down the state's debt, and not to build and support the retirement program that pays employee benefits during retirement.

In addition, the Texas teacher retirement health care fund is running out of money. The state will have to raise premiums and cut the benefits. The health care fund administrators have requested funds from the Texas legislature and have received $768 million to keep the health care system alive. There is only one way to fix this problem and that's to receive more money from the legislators, the member employees, and cut benefits.

The Teacher Retirement System is going broke...fast.

This means that all teachers must find other ways to have a better retirement program than the one the TRS system is barely providing.

TRS Benefits Are Getting Worse

With quickly rising healthcare costs and longer lifespans, state legislators have been reducing benefits for new teachers to the point that teachers starting out today are receiving a much worse compensation package than those who started before 2007.

If you are a teacher who was hired before 2007 and have at least five years' experience by 2014, you must meet the minimum age requirement of 60 in order to receive full retirement benefits. If you did not have five years of service credit by August 31, 2014, you must be at least 62 years old to receive full retirement benefits. Of course, if you meet the Rule of 80, you can still receive your retirement benefits but your benefits will be reduced by 5% for each year you are under age 60 or 62 as appropriate. If you were hired after 2007, you must be 62 and meet the rule of 80.

Let's refer to the same hypothetical example used above with the teacher named Joanne. She is 55 years old and has 33 years of experience. She met the Rule of 80 and was retiring with 75.9% of her pension, or $47,671. With the new rule, she needs to be 62 to retire with no deductions. Joanne is 55 and that is 7 years before her full retirement age of 62. This means that her pension will be reduced by 35% (7 yr. x 5%) or $16,684. The $47,671 became $30,986. It won't matter if you hate your job, or you get fired, or if you are sick; all teachers will be forced to work until age 62 in order to get full benefits.

The TRS pension plan is back-end loaded which means that benefits grow very slowly for the first 20 or 25 years and then they begin growing faster as teachers get closer to the usual retirement age. This is a big problem for a lot of teachers because most teachers leave the profession long before the benefits of accumulated cash become available. The state estimates that about half of all new teachers leave the profession in their first eight years, and two thirds of all teachers leave the profession after less than 20 years of service. The amount of money growing in their account is minuscule over these shorter ranges of time. TRS knows this and uses this fact to the system's advantage.

Teachers who plan to stay working in the TRS system for 35 or 40 years and work after age 62, will actually have a decent retirement. Other teachers with short and medium-term time in the TRS system will only receive meager retirement benefits when they finally comply with the Rule of 80. They would be far better off withdrawing or transferring their accumulated contributions out of the TRS system and into a better retirement plan than leaving their money in their TRS account.

In every way, teachers are getting the short end of the stick, both as employees and when they retire. This is just the beginning of a huge problem in retirement benefits for the people who work for the state of Texas. This is your wake-up call and you need to start working on your solution right now instead of trusting TRS to do it for you. Obviously, TRS is not capable, so it is foolish to expect them to help you with your financial future and your retirement needs. Now is the time to get out and make the choices that preserve and grow your wealth, before it is too late.

Ready to Retire

You are about to make many important decisions that will have an impact on the rest of your life. Retiring decisions and retirement options should be taken under careful consideration as you look at all your options. Many eligible retirees are not getting proper recommendations from agents who only care about their commission.

The following illustration (8.2) is the same example and numbers using 55-year old Joanne with 33 years of experience.

Retirement is for those who met the Rule of 80 and are eligible to retire and get full benefits. The Partial Lump Sum Option (PLSO) option is for those teachers and administrators who meet the Rule of 90, and for teachers who are in the Rule of 80 and are also grandfathered-in for this option like Joanne. The Rule of 90 is used only to see who is qualified to receive the PLSO option. With the PLSO benefit, Joanne can receive a portion of her retirement benefits in a lump sum if she wishes, but this option will lower her standard monthly benefits. Joanne can choose the PLSO amount or any of the five option amounts if she decides to have a beneficiary.

Example of a PLSO Payout with TRS (Figure 8.2)

Includes no additional service credit		TRS-Care Eligibility: Yes		
Retirement Payment Plans	No PLSO elected	PLSO equal to 12 months elected	PLSO equal to 24 months elected	PLSO equal to 36 months elected
Partial Lump Sum Option (PLSO)		$47.671,32	$95.342,64	$143.013,96
		Plus Reduced Lifetime Monthly Annuities As Follows		
Standard Annuity	$3.972,61	$3.624,61	$3.276,61	$2.928,61
Option 1	$3.579,72	$3.266,14	$2.952,55	$2.638,97
Option 2	$3.766,03	$3.436,13	$3.106,23	$2.776,32
Option 3	$3.958,71	$3.611,92	$3.265,14	$2.918,36
Option 4	$3.917,39	$3.574,23	$3.231,06	$2.887,90
Option 5	$3.670,69	$3.349,14	$3.027,59	$2.706,03
Option 6				

Financial advisors often recommend that eligible members select a partial lump sum distribution. In the example above, the maximum amount of PLSO Joanne can receive is the 36 months option totaling $143,013. This money can be withdrawn and transferred into a personal account like an IRA or tax-sheltered annuity (TSA). These are retirement accounts Joanne can control or leave to her beneficiaries once she dies. There really is no point giving full control of your money to TRS. If you should die prematurely, your pension would be gone. If Joanne were to select the PLSO of 36 months, her annuity would be reduced, in this example from $3,972.61 monthly to $2,928.61, which is a $1,044 difference.

Teachers should always consult with an outside financial advisor, an advisor that does not have a biased opinion about how to invest for retirement. Many retirees request a counseling appointment directly with TRS on their upcoming retirement. TRS is not allowed to advise any TRS member about what to do, and they will never recommend the lump sum rollover option because it is not helpful to TRS. Remember, like any corporation, TRS will always do what is in its own best interests, and not yours.

Below are 5 mistakes that I see many educators make that could cost them thousands of dollars.

5 Mistakes I Often See Teachers Make

Mistake #1:

The first mistake is using the PLSO option. Another mistake is transferring the PLSO money into an annuity with an income rider. (Read Chapter 9, "Beware of the Income Rider"). Shifting from a pension (the TRS) into a deferred pension and receiving almost the same amount of money 10 years later does not make any sense. Yet, this product is very popular with teachers. (See Figure 9.3)

There are also agents who offer this product but do not understand the product themselves. A mistake like this could cost you thousands of dollars in retirement money and death benefits. We have many other options available that much more beneficial than this income rider. (See Figure 11.1)

Mistake #2:

Imagine this scenario. A husband and wife are both teachers and they retire at the same time. Each of them picked Option 1 and select the other as their beneficiary. Even though they have two insurance policies, when one of them dies, the survivor receives their own pension plus the pension of the deceased spouse for the rest of his or her life.

However, the other insurance policy that was being paid for years cancels because the beneficiary is dead. Most likely, two years later, the survivor also dies. Now both pensions are terminated and their children would receive nothing, zero. According to statistics, husbands and wives only outlive each other by two years.

A better strategy is to buy insurance policies from an independent insurance company. This is what I call Option 6, acquiring life insurance outside the TRS system. For married couples or singles, Option 1 might not be the best choice.

Mistake #3:

Many teachers purchase supplemental insurance from inside the school setting. Supplemental insurance includes coverage for such things as cancer, disability, term insurance, and dental and vision insurance. Because the prices are low, and the money is deducted from your check automatically. Teachers don't pay taxes on the premiums, all of which sounds like a great idea.

The problem is that the schools change vendors every two or three years. Because it is a different insurance company, the original rates are never locked and renewals are at a higher rate. When you retire, most of these group supplemental insurance policies can't be converted to individual policies and those that are convertible go up in price.

Instead of playing games like these, you're better off buying supplemental insurance policies from an independent insurance company outside the school system, and lock-in that rate. When you do this, you're making a fiscally responsible decision that will last a very long time.

Mistake #4:

Some teachers buy a 403(b) to supplement their TRS pension. Investing in a tax-deferred retirement account is always a good idea, but investing in a 403(b) is not. A 403(b) is the most common choice among teachers because that's the only account that school district employees have access to as employees of a nonprofit organization. The friendly company representatives travel from school to school offering the 403(b) and now the 457. Teachers usually don't know any better, so they buy the hype and invest in the wrong retirement vehicle.

The 403(b) representatives are not allowed to talk about anything else; this is their sole product and they are fishing in a barrel. 403(b)s have high fees, limits on how much money you can invest, and you have virtually no control until age 59 ½. This is not a good option for you.

Instead, consider funding an after-tax account like a Roth IRA or an IUL from an independent insurance company outside the school. Please see the illustrations comparing an IUL vs. a Roth IRA and a 403(b). You'll clearly see the difference and know exactly what to do.

Mistake #5:

The TRS Care Medicare Advantage plan is the most expensive Medicare Advantage plan in Texas. At present, the monthly premium is $135 a month with a $500 deductible. Fees this high can put a strain on all retired teachers with fixed income.

Because TRS members have had TRS insurance for most of their lives, they are not aware of the outside competition and the better values they could have if they did some research. For example, HMOs have $0 premiums and PPOs are available in almost every area of the state with $0 or small monthly premiums. Even Medicare Supplements could be a better deal with more advantages than those offered by TRS-Care.

Many teachers are afraid that once they leave TRS, they will never be allowed to go back, but we have helped hundreds of TRS members switch from TRS into an independent plan and not one of them has ever asked to return to TRS. The TRS system is broken and it is continuing to get worse. We recommend you look for other plans in your county and compare the benefits. Even better, give us a call and we will help you find a much better plan than TRS.

If you are a member of TRS, you owe it to yourself, your family, and your financial future to learn all your options as soon as possible.

Summary

The lessons learned in this chapter are:

1. TRS is a bad pension plan and it is getting worse.
2. TRS is an even worse investment vehicle than a 403(b).
3. TRS is not your best choice for buying supplemental insurance.

4. TRS is a back-end loaded program, so people who leave the system early do not receive the full amount of money they already paid in.
5. TRS members are required to contribute 7.7% of their salary, but receive only 2.3% because the state has unfunded liabilities to pay. In effect, TRS members are paying for the state's debts.
6. TRS is the most expensive Medicare Advantage Plan in Texas.
7. TRS is quickly going broke.

Chapter 9
Beware of the Income Rider!

What Exactly is an "Income Rider"?

If you are transferring money out of your pension into an annuity with an income rider... Beware! If the agent promised you a bonus, or 7% per year, or doubling your account's value in 10 years, income for life, money you cannot outlive, it all sounds great...but walk away. Quickly! This could be a trap.

Most financial advisors and insurance agents are selling variable and fixed indexed annuities with income riders attached. The riders are being used as promotions in order to sell the insurance policies.

As you probably know, a "rider" in an insurance policy is an optional provision that either changes or adds to an insurance policy's terms. Riders can sometimes offer beneficial features, such as extra coverage, for an additional annual cost.

This "income rider" offers the guarantee of lifetime income, giving the policyholder an income stream for life.

These annuities with this Rider have become very popular.

"If it looks too good to be true, it probably is." This famous phrase has it correct. Unfortunately, advisors do not understand how this product works, and most retirees with an income rider in their annuity also don't fully understand the feature they are paying for.

Before the Income Rider

Annuitants purchase an annuity with a 7-year or 10-year surrender policy. They withdraw their funds and move that contract to a different company after the surrender period is over. The problem is that the company would lose a client and control of the money, which the company wants to avoid.

To prevent this, insurance companies became very creative. Every insurance company developed their own version of an income rider, and each company tried to outdo the other with special features that made their income rider look more attractive for annuitants. Sadly, many annuitants believed that the income rider was the answer to having lifetime income.

Here is a formula you need to understand:

Income Benefit Base Value x Lifetime Withdrawal Percentage = Your Lifetime Income Amount

Let's take a closer look and see why this is a bad idea.

An income benefit base, which is different from your account's true value, grows until you are ready to start receiving your retirement distribution payments. The insurance companies found a strategy that worked when they juiced-up the Income Benefit Base amount, also known as a Guaranteed Lifetime Withdrawal Benefit Base, which is what the annuitants cared about the most.

For example, insurance companies used a variety of strategies including offering 10% or 20% bonuses, and 7% guaranteed income per year without any market risk. This was misleading because the 7% was referring to the growth of your benefit base at a 7% annual interest rate from your income rider, and not your actual account's value. Annuitants believe these numbers are great, and they forget about the Lifetime Withdrawal Percentage which is most important.

Annuitants didn't realize that the benefit base isn't real money. Many of them thought that the base money was money they would be able to walk away with and believed the 7% interest rate was their real account value.

Unfortunately, the retirees didn't pay attention to the Lifetime

Withdrawal Percentage which decides the total amount of lifetime income a retiree will receive through the income rider.

While enhancing the Benefit Base, the Lifetime Withdrawal Percentage was reduced. This withdrawal percentage is usually based on your age and gender. The longer you wait to receive your withdrawals, the higher the percentage will be. The Lifetime Income is calculated when the Base Value is multiplied by the Lifetime Withdrawal Percentage.

All riders have a fee, and these fees can be very expensive. Because the insurance companies want to make sure they don't lose the money in the account, the withdrawal percentage is reduced to balance the scale. This way, distribution payouts can take between 20-25 years before the recipient taps into the insurance company's money. If there's a joint payout or a younger annuitant, it might take even more years. Have you checked your mortality table?

The insurance company is banking on you not living long enough to get your money paid back to you so they can make a profit by holding onto your money as long as possible.

Each withdrawal amount is reduced from the real accumulation value, and if there is a balance on that amount, the balance is given to the beneficiaries.

Another problem with income riders is that the true account does not grow very much. That's because the rider fees eat up the value in the real account. In many cases, once the income starts, the actual contract values stop growing. Prospects and clients never see the real account illustrations so they don't know how the insurance company is using the situation to its advantage. If you happen to have this product, call the insurance company. Find out the real account value and the interest rate that is being credited. It is probably around 2%.

Here is an illustration of a teacher named Linda who is going to receive a pension. Linda's former advisor recommended an income rider with her lump sum withdrawal. Transferring a teacher pension to another pension-like account is not a good idea.

Example of a PLSO Payout with TRS (Figure 9.1)

Includes no additional service credit		TRS-Care Eligibility: Yes		
Retirement Payment Plans	No PLSO elected	PLSO equal to 12 months elected	PLSO equal to 24 months elected	PLSO equal to 36 months elected
Partial Lump Sum Option (PLSO)		$47.671,32	$95.342,64	**$143.013,96**
		Plus Reduced Lifetime Monthly Annuities As Follows		
Standard Annuity	**$3.972,61**	$3.624,61	$3.276,61	**$2.928,61**
Option 1	$3.579,72	$3.266,14	$2.952,55	$2.638,97
Option 2	$3.766,03	$3.436,13	$3.106,23	$2.776,32
Option 3	$3.958,71	$3.611,92	$3.265,14	$2.918,36
Option 4	$3.917,39	$3.574,23	$3.231,06	$2.887,90
Option 5	$3.670,69	$3.349,14	$3.027,59	$2.706,03
Option 6				

In the illustration above, Linda transferred money from her pension of $143,013.96. Her standard annuity was reduced from $3,972.61 to $2,928.61. This is a decrease of $1,044 each month, which is a lot of money to lose.

The table below (9.2) is a list of some of the many income rider choices companies offer. As you can see, we have the best performing income riders in the market today.

Comparison of Rider Choices of Different Companies (Figure 9.2)

		Guaranteed Income Rider Comparison						
Yrs	Age	8% Bonus	6% Bonus	No Bonus	No Bonus	No Bonus	12% Bonus	No Bonus
0	62	7,413	0	6,364	8,068	6,521	0	7,722
1	63	8,097	7,217	7,157	9,025	7,597	8,408	8,180
2	64	8,841	7,983	7,979	9,621	8,877	8,829	8,649
3	65	10,122	8,820	8,830	10,285	9,970	10,197	9,129
4	66	11,033	9,736	9,710	10,423	11,266	10,707	9,621
5	67	12,022	10,630	10,618	11,047	12,106	11,243	11,390
6	68	13,095	11,715	11,554	11,322	12,919	11,805	11,926
7	69	14,260	13,022	12,520	11,809	13,308	12,395	12,474
8	70	15,683	14,324	13,514	13,100	15,097	14,198	13,138
9	71	16,894	15,606	14,536	13,404	16,256	14,908	13,712
10	72	18,380	16,996	15,587	14,060	17,332	15,653	16,602
11	73	18,871	17,488	16,667	14,500	18,000	15,810	17,234
12	74	19,370	17,993	17,775	14,814	18,504	15,968	17,878
13	75	20,659	19,302	18,912	15,826	18,729	17,471	18,807
14	76	21,182	20,011	20,077	16,155	19,135	17,646	19,479
15	77	21,713	20,741	21,271	16,483	19,910	17,822	20,163
16	78	22,252	21,491	22,494	17,183	20,476	18,001	20,449

The chart above also shows which companies return the highest annual income based on the year the person chooses to activate their income rider. If you ever need to purchase an income rider, we are able to show you which companies are performing the best and which will give you the highest Lifetime Income Amount.

Three examples follow that demonstrate the situation faced by Linda, the teacher. For this example, we use the highest performing Income Rider in the market today.

Option A: Income Rider

Linda, at 62, was going to transfer $143,013 to an annuity with Income Rider attached. Her teacher pension was reduced to $2,928 per month. Ten years later, at 72, she was going to receive $18,380 per year or $1,531 per month for the rest of her life. Please keep in mind that the life expectancy for a female is 86, which means there were only going to be 14 years of benefits for her. Insurance companies rarely use their own funds to fund accounts. The actual account value probably grew at a low rate of 1.5%. After 10 year, at this rate, it would have grown to $165.977. After withdrawal of $18,380 per year it will only last 10 year and would have $0 death benefits.

Option B: Invest Yourself

Instead of moving the money out of Linda's pension, this option uses the difference of $1,044 a month and invests it. Her teacher pension stayed at $3,972 per month, not $2,928. Investing this $1,044 per month at a fixed rate of 3.5% for a 10-year period will result in the accumulation of $151,224. Please remember Linda is receiving $3,972 monthly from the pension, so all that's needed is an additional $487.66 per month to match the $1,531.66 from the income rider (Option 1).

The $151,224 yielding 3.5% will be used to withdraw $487.66 per month. The calculation is $1,044 + $487 = $1,531 and there is still $151,224 in the account. This is a much better outcome than the income rider. To match the income rider amount of $18,380 in monthly extra benefits, this option will still have $69,297 after 16 years as a death benefit.

Option C: Index Product

The third option is my favorite. Linda's advisor can move the $143,013 to a very popular index product with no rider. In this hypothetical illustration, after 10 years the account will be $313,882. This amount is $162,658 ($313,882 - $151,224) more than Option B. With the $313,882, Linda can withdraw $18,380 (the rider amount) per year forever.

The interest on this account is much greater than the withdrawal amount, therefore the account value and death benefit are increasing. The withdrawal amounts could increase or decrease to meet the annuitant's needs. Not only do you have many options with this product, but it will also help leave a legacy for your loved ones. Your beneficiaries will receive the annuity's full account value after death.

The chart below (9.3) will help you better understand all three options by comparing apples to apples.

Income Rider Comparison (Figure 9.3)

	Income Rider		Invest $1041		Index Investment
	Option 1		Option 2		Option 3
Age 62/Mth	$ 2,928		$ 3,972,000		$ 2,928
Roll Over	$ 143,013	Invest	$1041 x 3.5%	Roll Over	$ 143,013
Age 72	$2,928 +		$3972 +		$2,928 +
	$1,531 =		$487 =		$1,531 =
Monthly Benefit	$4.459,00		$4.459,00		$4.459,00
Estimated			$1041/Mth +		
Walk Away Value	$ 165,977		151,224		$ 313,882
Age 86 (Dead)	$0 monthly		$0 monthly		$0 monthly
Death Benefit	$ 0		$ 69,297		$500,000 +

It is easy to see how a simple fixed account can perform better than the annuity with the income rider. Obviously, Option 3 the Index Investment is the best. Mathematics don't lie. Why would anybody want an income rider after seeing this example?

The illustration below was used for information for Option 3, the index product. It is not the S&P 500 which has low caps and small participation percentages. This new alternative index uses volatility control and higher caps than the well-known S&P 500.

This illustration uses the performance of the last 20 years and it is NOT a guarantee. This fixed product is used when transferring or rolling over other accounts like 401(k)s, IRAs or 403(b)s. The account in this illustration continues to grow in value even after the withdrawals start.

Option 3: Index Annuity – Non-Guarantee (Figure 9.4)

Year	Age	Withdrawal	Rate	Credit	Value
0	62	$ 0	0.00%	$ 0	$ 143,013
1	63	$ 0	12.93%	$ 18,489	$ 161,502
2	64	$ 0	11.80%	$ 19,054	$ 180,556
3	65	$ 0	10.82%	$ 19,542	$ 200,097
4	66	$ 0	12.88%	$ 25,765	$ 225,862
5	67	$ 0	14.35%	$ 32,413	$ 258,275
6	68	$ 0	0.41%	$ 1,051	$ 259,326
7	69	$ 0	3.35%	$ 8,682	$ 268,009
8	70	$ 0	8.80%	$ 23,593	$ 291,601
9	71	$ 0	0.00%	$ 0	$ 291,601
10	72	$ 14,580	13.31%	$ 36,860	$ 313,882
11	73	$ 15,694	12.93%	$ 38,550	$ 336,737
12	74	$ 16,837	11.80%	$ 37,742	$ 357,642
13	75	$ 17,882	10.82%	$ 36,772	$ 376,533
14	76	$ 18,380	12.88%	$ 46,116	$ 404,268
15	77	$ 18,380	14.35%	$ 55,379	$ 441,267
16	78	$ 18,380	0.41%	$ 1,721	$ 424,608
17	79	$ 18,380	3.35%	$ 13,601	$ 419,829
18	80	$ 18,380	8.80%	$ 35,340	$ 436,788
19	81	$ 18,380	0.00%	$ 0	$ 418,408
20	82	$ 18,380	13.31%	$ 53,228	$ 453,256
30	92	$ 0	13.31%	$ 106,056	$ 903,106

Clients are unfamiliar with the details of riders and often do not understand what they are doing and how they are limiting their retirement income when signing up for this product. Frankly, they are not supposed to know. They don't do the math correctly. This is the reason why they hire advisors, because they trust us to help them with this very important life-changing decision. I have never seen any advisor or YouTube video break-down the income rider the way that I just did.

Agents offer bonuses, 7% guarantees, and income for life, but they don't talk about the real account value. The rider fees and the withdrawals will eat-up and empty the account fast. It's not the fault of the insurance companies, but rather the agents who don't understand what they are selling or are only thinking about themselves and their commission.

Income riders are not good for most retirees. This product might be good for somebody who has millions of dollars in a 401(k) and does not have a lifetime income account, or somebody who is not receiving Social Security or a pension and wants to have a portion of his retirement warranted for life, but never the whole account.

Receiving the lump sum from a pension and using that money to start another pension-like product is not a good idea. Of course, it's hard to understand this when thousands of financial advisors are recommending this product.

I do recommend withdrawing money from pensions when given the opportunity because of several reasons. Once you start a pension, you can't change the outcome. Obviously, having money you can control for emergencies or other investments is always the best choice. In addition, if a premature death occurs, the money will go to the client's heirs and not remain with the company. Option 3, above, is recommended as the best option for most types of rollovers or transfers.

If you believe you have one of these accounts or something similar, we can still help and we can still find other alternatives.

Summary

1. Don't transfer money out of a pension to start an Annuity with an Income Rider.
2. Guarantees are usually never the best option.
3. There are many other options better than an Annuity with an Income Rider.
4. If you are rolling over or transferring accounts, find an experience honest agent who can break down and compare the different investment opportunities.
5. The illustration in Chapter 11 (Figure 11.1) consists of other index options that should be considered.

Chapter 10
Be A Bank ... and Make Money

Do you have any or know any misconceptions when it comes to money? Here are a few inaccurate beliefs I hear a lot. Credit cards are evil. A 30-year mortgage is a bad idea. I don't need life insurance; all debt is a bad. These misconceptions are part of the reason why people incorrectly make the wrong decisions when it comes to money and investments. These views or opinions are because of something that you learned a long time ago, something that your parents said or a television commercial you saw. Even so-called expects who get paid lots of money to give advice are misleading consumers and feed incorrect information. This chapter is based on the idea that debt is good and explains how people can use debt to build personal wealth and become millionaires.

Most people believe what they have been taught about debt. Dave Ramsey tells everybody to pay off all their debt as soon as possible. Debt is bad. Debt is evil. Debt erodes your financial worth. Everybody hates debt because of what they have been taught. If given a choice, most people would rather not have debt. People think being debt-free is the ideal, but this is not how banks do business. Banks love debt and grow more and more financially powerful because of their debt. This is something you can do, too. Let's learn why banks are so successful and see if there is anything we can do to increase our wealth just like the banks.

When you ask kids what they want to be when they grow up, most kids will say they want to be a teacher, a doctor, a lawyer, or have their own business. No one ever says, "I want to be a bank." It may sound silly to say this, but why not?

The idea of becoming your own bank might seem surprising, but you can do this in a small way and enjoy the big financial benefits banks do. Hold your disbelief for a moment and let me explain this concept to you.

Let me ask you a question. Which would you rather have?

Option A: No debt and no retirement money.

Option B: $100,000 debt and $200,000 in your retirement account.

My goal is to show you how to obtain Option B.

Before we take another step, I'd like to clear something up right away. What interest percentage rate are you making in your investments? If you don't have any investments such as stocks, 401(k), mutual funds, IRAs or IULs earning at least 8%, then all debt is bad debt and you should pay it off.

Whether or not your debt is good or bad depends on what your investments are yielding in interest. To earn money like a bank, you need to have, or start, an investment that averages at least 8% return on your investment. People who understand the concept of money and how interest works know how to use this strategy to maximize their investment and manage their good debt. Many 20-years olds are borrowing money at any interest rate and using that money to trade stock. They are trying to become overnight millionaires with borrowed money. That is a different book. My recommending are to borrow at a low interest rate and get a tax-free investment with zero risk and not stocks.

You don't need any special ability or a high IQ. You simply need to understand the basics of compound interest and put that to work for you. Learning to make money is very simple when you know what you're doing. Banks have perfected the art of borrowing good debt with low interest so they can earn high interest with the money they are borrowing.

One of the best ways to be successful is to imitate what successful people and profitable companies do. If banks are the most successful and wealthiest industry in the world, then we should be copying what banks do so we can be successful and wealthy, too.

What Do Banks Do?

That's simple. They borrow lots and lots of money from you and me. They have debt, lots of debt, and they always want to borrow more money. You've never heard of a bank calling up their customers and asking if they want their money back. You've never heard of a bank that encourages withdrawals. Have you? No, of course not.

The wealthiest businesses in the world, such as banks and insurance companies, love to be in debt.

Let me say this one more time. Debt is good only if you have good investments.

What's a good investment? A good investment is making more interest with the investment than what you are paying in interest on the money that you owe. This is the law that banks live by. They borrow money at a lower rate and use that money to earn a higher rate. Smart! How can you make this work for yourself? You need to find a good investment that yields more interest than what you're paying for the debt.

Banks are paying 1% to 2% on CDs and hardly anything on savings accounts. Making 1% or 2% interest won't even beat inflation, which averages about 3% a year. People who own these kinds of savings accounts are losing their buying power and are not staying even with the constantly rising costs of life. Meanwhile, the banks are using this borrowed money to make personal loans to people like you and me at 8%, and even 12% or higher. This is how banks are making billions of dollars by using our money.

Even though banks are making a fortune on loaning money at high interest rates, banks also have to offer low interest rate loans for cars at 2% or 4%, and they are restricted in the amount of interest they can charge for mortgages, which is currently around 4%. Even right now, because of the COVID-19 epidemic and with all the efforts to revive the economy, low interest loans are available at around 3.5%. That's because the Federal Reserve controls these kinds of interest rates to stabilize the national economy. Only a few people will take advantage of this opportunity for borrowing at a low interest to build their own personal wealth.

Lower interest rates allow people to afford the purchase of homes or cars, so when people can access lower interest rates for big money items like these, more people will buy and that helps the economy improve and grow. However, even if it is a 2% loan, banks are still making more interest than what they're paying. Banks never make a loan without making money on that loan.

Think about credit card companies for a moment. These companies are owned by banks and they are lending our money anywhere from 8% to 28%. Now you can see why banks are getting bigger and richer all the time. They are always making more interest than what they are paying out. This is their rule for financial success.

How About You and Me?

What if we became a bank and do what the banks are doing? The richest, most successful and smartest people in the world have debt. They even borrow money when they don't have to.

Take Donald Trump for example. The 45th President of the United States has lots of debt. In August 2016, Trump's outstanding debt was around $650 million, and that's in addition to an outstanding loan of $950 million from the Bank of China.

Yet, President Trump's net worth in 2018 was around $3.1 billion. Donald Trump is considered one of the richest people in the country and he has tons of debt. He launched an empire by taking on large loans, and with this money he built many luxury hotels, apartments, and casinos which have all become iconic monuments. This never would have happened if he had not taken loans and accepted good debt.

Donald Trump did not borrow millions of dollars to build his towers and pay off the loans as quickly as possible. Instead, Trump borrowed at a low interest rate and did not pay-off the principal. He doesn't want to pay-off the loans. The equity in his buildings and property is still increasing because the appraised value is growing all the time. Instead, he is paying the minimum payment possible and waiting until the very last day to make his required payments. Trump wants debt because the debt is in his favor.

Why can't we do that? We should be copying the wealthiest and smartest people by doing what they do.

Of course, I realize we can't go out and buy a bank. Most of us will never be in a situation where we can make 12% or 18% like banks and other financial institutions do. Not everyone is able to borrow millions of dollars from the Bank of China, or build hotels and casinos. However, what we can do is borrow from banks and other institutions that offer low interest rates between 2% to 4%.

The First Step

The first step for becoming successful the way a bank is successful is to change the way we think. All our lives, we have been trained by our parents and society to believe that debt is bad. Everything you read tells you to pay-off your mortgage as soon as possible. Many advisers tell us to make extra payments to the principal to eliminate the debt quickly. We are warned not to get college loans. We should pay off every loan as soon as possible. This advice is everywhere, but it's not the best advice. Everyone worries about the total interest they will have to pay instead of looking at the Big Picture and properly managing the investment they've created. But now you know better.

The Second Step

The second step is a must. In order to imitate the success of a bank, you have to have, or have to establish, an investment account that yields an average of 6% or higher.

If you already have an investment account earning 6% or higher, perfect. If you don't have one, my recommendation is to start an Index Universal

Life insurance policy (IUL). Creating this type of account is the beginning and the foundation of a great investment. You don't have to be a genius or do anything special to make this work for you and your family. It's a simple process that takes a little time and a little effort to set-up and then it runs by itself. (Read Chapter 5 on IULs.)

The Third Step

The third step is something most people don't want to do, and that is to create debt. You'll want to borrow money at a low interest rate through such loans as mortgages, car loans, or student loans. Get a long-term loan and only pay the minimum payment, even if you can afford to pay more. The idea is to place your extra money into the investment that's earning you 6% or more in return. You're borrowing money with a low interest loan and putting your extra money to work for you in your IUL.

This is why we need to change the way we think. Numbers never lie, and if you follow this strategy, you will steadily build wealth using the bank's money. Let the bank work for you instead of the other way around.

Another Example

Let's remember the main idea. Banks don't worry about how much interest they pay because they are making a lot more interest using the money they borrow. They make 8% or higher and pay out 2%. This is a sweet deal for them, and it could be a sweet deal for you, too.

Here's another way to understand this concept. For about 28 years I've had a very nice cleaning lady come to my house to wash, iron, and clean my house. People always ask me why I don't wash and iron and clean the house myself. They tell me I could do it slowly while I watch television, and I'd save a lot of money. What they say is true.

However, this is always my response. "You want me to spend my whole Saturday washing, ironing and cleaning my house, hating every minute of it, just to save $1,00? Do you know how many sales I can do in one day?" When I pay my cleaning lady $100 for the day, I can go play golf in the morning and make a few business appointments for that afternoon. If I make one Medicare Advantage sale that day I can make $255 or more, just on that one sale. Here are the mathematics: I pay $100 and I make $255, so I am making more than what I am paying out. Every time I do this, I am profiting by a difference of $155, at least.

This is what banks do. They pay a little but earn more.

We need to change our thinking and forget what we think we know about money. Instead of focusing and worrying about how much interest we're paying, we should concentrate on how much interest we're making by keeping our debt. Instead of paying-off low interest loans, you could be building your financial portfolio by paying the minimum payments and depositing the extra money into your IUL or other investments. The typical plan of paying the mortgage first, or paying off the student loan or car loan first and only then beginning an investment never works out. You will always find another car to buy and another vacation to take. There will always be taxes, insurance and debt you have to pay off. That future investment you plan in the future will never even begin

Example of a 30-Year Mortgage

Most people don't want a mortgage that lasts for 30 years. They look at the total interest being paid over the course of a 30-year period. It looks very scary, so they react in fear and choose to pay off their debt early. This is a big mistake, as you can now see. Instead of paying off the loan early, they can use that money as additional investment money in their IUL. Let's look at this example.

Instead of taking a 15-year $200,000 mortgage with a rate of 4% and a payment of $1,479, Janie took out a 30-year mortgage. The same mortgage in a 30-year loan is $955. The difference between the two terms is $524 per month. Janie also commits to contributing the remaining $524 a month to start and build her IUL investment.

Immediately, the IUL provides Janie with a $606,000 death benefit that every young family needs. Then, after 15 years, the cash value in her IUL will be greater than the balance she owes on her 30-year mortgage.

If Janie chooses, she can pay-off her mortgage and still have cash value in her IUL policy. Of course, paying-off a low interest loan in this book is not recommended, but she has this option if she wishes.

Using this option of a 30-year loan and depositing the difference in her IUL is an example of how many of today's money problems can be solved. Janie's IUL provides life insurance, and a cash value that could be used as loans for a new car, to send her children to college, for use in emergencies, to purchase long term care, and even provide retirement income. Remember that Janie's withdrawals are all tax-free as well. Illustrations are available.

Student Loans

When funds are needed for college, get student loans when possible. Don't use your own money to pay for college. Most student loans are deferred until after graduation. Also, the interest rate on these loans is from between 2% to 5%, which makes them a very good loan. The rule is to pay off the minimum payment only and use the extra income to fund your IUL, which is earning an average return of 8% interest.

Car Loans

It's the same thing with the car loan. Lots of people will save their money in a bank, which of course is a losing proposition. Then they will wait until they have enough money to buy a brand-new car. They'd rather do this than make low interest payments, so of course they are shooting themselves in the foot and using their money improperly. Instead of paying back the loan quickly, they should make minimum payments and place the difference in their investment, which is earning a higher rate of interest.

Many of today's car loans have a rate as low as 0%. Your money should be working for you and not to pay-off a low interest loan like this. This strategy is different from what most people are used to doing. It's hard to believe your eyes when everybody else and all of society is preaching the opposite practice.

A mortgage, a student loan, and a car loan are all good examples of how you can implement this strategy and imitate the banks. This does not require you being a genius. Instead, trust mathematics and learn how to manage your finances. If you don't yet have an investment that's earning an average of 6% or higher, now is the time to get one.

Opportunities to borrow money at a lower rate come up all the time. For example, because of the present COVID-19 pandemic, the Small Business Administration (SBA) was offering loans to small companies in order to help stimulate the economy. Loans were distributed at a low interest of 3.5% and I borrowed $150,000. Also since mortgage rate decreased, I got a home equity loan. I kept the monthly payment the same and received $52,000 out my house. People who understand how money works will take this opportunity to make other investments and earn higher interest. I will let you know my results in the next book.

Other books have their own version of how to "be your own bank". They borrow from the IUL cash value instead of from the bank. This strategy works, too, but only after years of investing when you have cash accumulated in your IUL. Paying 5% (the loan rate) and making an average of 8% in the IUL is great. However, "being a bank" is much better. Borrow from a bank at a lower rate of 2 - 4% and making 8%. Using bank's or other people's money is much better. Numbers don't lie.

My recommendations are to borrow at an interest rate less than 5% and not at 8%-12%. If you decide on

Anyone can become a millionaire. You can do this, too. All you have to do is get a job, get low interest rate loans, and save your money in your 8% interest account every month. I am not recommending to borrowing at a rate of 8% or 12% like many people who I advise are doing. The reason why they borrow at 8% or 12% is because these people have accounts that are making 20% or more. With plenty of time, they let compound interest do the work for them and concentrate in building the retirement accounts at higher rates. Now that you have this knowledge about how to rearrange your finances, making money is actually very simple.

Most people are very skeptical when it comes to money. They worry about paying off their debt instead of finding ways to build-up their investments. They lack financial education, and don't know how to make their own money work for them.

The important thing is to be consistent and committed. When you change your beliefs and think about money, you open the door to a lifetime of financial prosperity.

Summary

The lessons learned in this chapter are:

1. Good debt can be your friend; bad debt is your enemy.
2. Borrowing money at a low interest rate and using the borrowed funds to earn a higher interest rate is what banks do...and so can you.
3. Mortgages, car loans, and student loans are examples of good debt because the interest rates are low.

Chapter 11
Examples of IULs

Our company does not focus only on IULs and Roth IRAs. We offer a wide variety of products to meet all your financial needs, even Medicare plans. Our company is independent and we work with the best investment companies that offer superior products. We can bring you the highest quality financial products and services for the growth of your investment portfolio, and assist you with achieving the security of a comfortable retirement lifestyle.

The investment products we offer are an excellent fit for any 401(k) and IRA transfer or rollover. We are also experts who can help you get started with a traditional IRA, a Roth IRA, or a 403(b) as necessary. No single investment product will serve all your financial needs, so a personal evaluation is necessary to help us precisely tailor our recommendations and customize our services for you.

The company and product used for the illustration below is the same as the one shown in Chapter 8, "Beware of the Income Rider". The index used in the chart was the alternative index because it controls volatility and contains higher annual caps. Normally the S&P 500 Index has low caps and a low participation percentage.

In this illustration the product is fixed, guaranteed to never go below 0%, and it specializes in accumulation. With this product you also get home health care, nursing care, terminal illness, and wealth transfer benefits. All are included with no extra fees. This hybrid index has become very popular and has replaced the older conservative low-performing indices.

The chart bellow also shows historical data for each year during the most recent 20-year period. The Return Index Selection shows the return with the current Cap Rate, Participation Rate, and a $0 floor. Zero is the Hero! See the illustration below on the S&P 500.

The illustration shows one product in three different contract ranges:

Comparison of 7-year, 10-year, and 14-year Contracts (Figure 11.1)

		7-year contract			10-year			14-year	
YEAR	AGE	CREDIT RATE	CREDIT AMOUNT	VALUE	CREDIT RATE	CREDIT AMOUNT	VALUE	CREDIT RATE	VALUE
0	60			$100.000			$100.000		$100.000
1	61	10,54%	$10.538	$110.538	10,94%	$110.936	$110.936	12,93%	$112.928
2	62	9,56%	$10.565	$121.103	9,93%	$121.954	$121.954	11,80%	$126.251
3	63	8,71%	$10.553	$131.656	9,07%	$133.009	$133.009	10,82%	$139.915
4	64	10,49%	$13.813	$145.470	10,89%	$147.494	$147.494	12,88%	$157.931
5	65	11,77%	$17.123	$162.593	12,20%	$165.490	$165.490	14,35%	$180.596
6	66	0,00%	$0	$162.593	0,00%	$165.490	$165.490	0,41%	$181.331
7	67	2,23%	$3.632	$166.225	2,42%	$169.495	$169.495	3,35%	$187.402
8	68	6,96%	$11.573	$177.798	7,27%	$181.815	$181.815	8,80%	$203.899
9	69	0,00%	$0	$177.798	0,00%	$181.815	$181.815	0,00%	$203.899
10	70	10,87%	$19.318	$197.115	11,27%	$202.309	$202.309	13,31%	$231.029
20	80	10,87%	$38.078	$388.545	11,27%	$409.291	$409.291	13,31%	$533.745
30	90	10,87%	$75.058	$765.881	11,27%	$828.034	$828.034	13,31%	$1.233.108

7, 10, and 14 years. The lower the contract year, the lower the cap rate or participation percentage. You can see that after 10 years, the 7-year contract almost doubled and the 10-year and 14-year contracts more than doubled their value amount. This chart represents an average based on past performance and is not intended to predict future performance. If you wish to see comparisons or illustrations for this product, they are available for your review.

S&P 500 Index Performance

Let's focus now on Indexed Universal Life (IUL). The chart below shows the past performance of the actual S&P 500 Index for the last 21 years. The credited amounts are shown for accounts starting on January 1 and ending December 31 of each year. The other two columns are IULs with two different allocations, one with an Annual Point to Point (PTP) and a cap of 10%. The column on the right shows a PTP with no cap and a 6.3% margin (fee).

In this example, if it was possible to invest straight into the S&P 500 Index with no caps and no floor, the $100,000 investment would have grown to $267,914 in the 21 years. Look closely and you'll see that the S&P 500 Index did not grow at all during the 10 years between 1999 and 2009. The $100,000 investment lost -11% and decreased to $89,479.

S&P 500 Index PTP Comparisons (Figure 11.2)

End Year	S&P 500* Index Change	S&P 500* $ 100,00 Investment	S&P 500* Annual Point to Point 10% Cap	S&P 500* Annual Point to Point $ 100,00 Investment	S&P 500* Annual PTP w/Spread 6,3% No Cap	S&P 500* Annual PTP w/Spread 6,3% $ 100,00 Investment
1999	19,5%	119.500,00	10	110.000,00	13,2%	113.200,00
2000	-12,7%	104.323,00	0	110.000,00	0,0%	113.200,00
2001	-13,0%	90.761,00	0	110.000,00	0,0%	113.200,00
2002	-23,4%	69.523,00	0	110.000,00	0,0%	113.200,00
2003	26,4%	87.877,00	10	121.000,00	20,1%	135.953,00
2004	9,0%	95.786,00	9	131.890,00	2,7%	139.624,00
2005	4,7%	100.288,00	4.7	138.088,00	0,0%	139.624,00
2006	13,5%	113.827,00	10	151.897,00	7,2%	149.677,00
2007	3,5%	117.811,00	3.5	157.214,00	0,0%	149.677,00
2008	-38,5%	72.453,00	0	157.214,00	0,0%	149.677,00
2009	23,5%	89.479,00	10	172.935,00	17,2%	175.421,00
2010	12,.8%	100.932,00	10	190.229,00	6,5%	186.823,00
2011	1,5%	102.446,00	1.5	193.082,00	0,0%	186.823,00
2012	13,4%	116.174,00	10	212.390,00	7,1%	200.088,00
2013	29,6%	150.562,00	10	233.629,00	23,3%	146.708,00
2014	11,4%	167.726,00	10	256.993,00	5,1%	259.290,00
2015	-0,7%	166.552,00	0	256.993,00	0,0%	259.290,00
2016	10,5%	184.040,00	10	282.692,00	4,2%	270.181,00
2017	20,4%	221.584,00	10	310.961,00	14,1%	308.276,00
2018	-6,2%	207.846,00	0	310.961,00	0,0%	308.276,00
2019	28,9%	267.914,00	10	342.057,00	22,6%	377.943,00

Now compare this result with the IUL and you'll see that from the same time period between 1999 to 2009, the PTP with the 10% cap account grew to $172,935 and the margin account grew to $175,421. This is a huge difference compared with the performance of the actual S&P 500 Index. This is why we keep repeating "Zero is the Hero".

At the end of 2019, the PTP account had grown to $342,057 while the spread account grew even higher to $377,943, a difference of +27% and +41% respectively during the same period of time. Which account would you choose if you could?

The difference in the performance of the regular S&P 500 index account and the PTP accounts is that the PTP accounts had a $0 floor, which means the account holder never lost a dime. Meanwhile, the true S&P 500 Index had three very big negative years, making it very hard to regain losses even with large gains later. Having a $0 floor is a tremendous benefit because the policyholder can't lose money!

Time Is Important

As you realize by now, delaying financial investment could cost you thousands, if not millions, of potential dollars. Procrastination is the most damaging thing you can do when it comes to your retirement investments. The sooner you open an IUL for yourself and your children, the better it will be for all of you and the faster it will compound.

Illustrations

Now let's turn our focus to the charts. All illustrations below use a conservative 6.27% annual rate of return. The same rate of return is being used for the other products we are comparing with.

For a Newborn

To give you a crystal-clear picture, the next illustration compares an IUL with a Roth IRA, which is also a tax-free account. The difference is astounding.

Comparison of a Roth IRA with an IUL for a Newborn (Figure 11.3)

			Roth IRA		Index Universal Life (IUL)		
			1 Cash Withdrawal	2 Account Value	1 Policy Loan	2 Surrender Value*	3 Death Benefit
Yr	Age	Deposit					
1	0	900	0	908	0	0	200,463
22	21	900	0	34,262	0	25,728	225,728
23	22	1,500	0	37,457	0	28,991	228,991
41	40	1,500	20,000	111,052	20,000	133,097	364,382
60	59	1,500	0	329,100	0	592,294	813,365
		76,800	20,000		20,000		
61	60	0	62,185	310,483	62,185	571,202	780,560
62	61	0	62,185	261,227	62,185	549,679	759,352
63	62	0	62,185	209,407	62,185	527,717	736,581
64	63	0	62,185	154,888	62,185	505,389	712,179
65	64	0	62,185	97,530	62,185	482,707	685,981
66	65	0	62,185	37,185	62,185	459,767	657,908
67	66	0	37,185	0	62,185	436,564	638,358
90	89	0	0	0	62,185	140,114	397,262
91	90	0	0	0	62,185	151,487	426,141
92	91	0	0	0	0	236,799	471,600
		76,800	430,295		1,947,735		

As a newborn, Sarah's parents or grandparents start her account with monthly payments of $75 (annual $900) and then increase the premiums to $125 per month by the time Sarah is age 23. It is always a good idea to increase the monthly premium later in life, or increase the death benefit, to allow higher deposits. At age 40 and 59, Sarah withdrew $20,000. At age 60, Sarah withdrew $62,185 per year. In this example, Sarah's Roth IRA would run out of money by age 67, but notice that Sarah's IUL is still going strong even at age 90. In the IUL, a cash value and the death benefit are both still available, even after Sarah's entire lifetime.

Parents and grandparents should help their children or grandchildren by creating investment portfolios while remaining the owners of the policy until the child is ready to take ownership as an adult. The Roth IRA requires income, but the IUL does not, and no medical exam is required. The child just needs to be born healthy. The cost of insurance is low and most of the money paid into the account will go toward the cash value.

Time is the key. While parents may have 30 or 40 years until retirement, a child who starts early could have 60 or more years of investment growth, all completely tax-free. With an IUL, there is no reason to consider Roth IRAs or 529 accounts ("qualified tuition plans"). This is a perfect example of how time is so important and why you should always start early. This is the greatest and best gift a parent could ever give their children. Financial independence is a blessing.

For a 25-Year Old

Most 25-year-olds or college graduates want to pay off their college loans as soon as possible or buy a new car and a mortgage. Most of them will never even think about opening a retirement account unless they are fortunate enough to have smart parents who have set-up the account for them.

The illustration below is a comparison of a 25-year-old's investment in a Roth IRA and an IUL. To make the comparison clear, the annual contribution for both is $6,000 with a 6.27% rate of interest.

Comparison of a Roth IRA with an IUL for a 25-year Old (Figure 11.4)

| | | | Roth IRA/Non Taxable | | Index Universal Life (IUL) | | |
| | | | 1 Cash Withdrawal | 2 Account Value | 1 Cash Withdrawal | 2 Account Value | 3 Death Benefit |
Yr	Age	Deposit	Withdrawal	Value	Withdrawal	Value	Benefit
1	25	6,000	0	6,300	0	0	405,145
2	26	6,000	0	12,915	0	3,211	410,621
20	44	6,000	0	208,316	0	210,520	610,52
30	54	6,000	0	418,565	0	501,638	901,638
34	58	6,000	0	535,922	0	685,162	1,085,162
35	59	6,000	0	569,018	0	739,258	1,139,258
36	60	0	68,897	525,127	68,897	718,068	1,118,068
46	70	0	16,962	0	68,897	498,495	898,495
47	71	0	0	0	68,897	477,356	877,356
65	89	0	0	0	68,897	360,171	760,171
66	90	0	0	0	68,897	381,495	781,495
67	91	0	0	0	0	479,482	879,482
68	92	0	0	0	0	584,716	984,716
		210,000	705,932		2,135,807		

Contributions were made until age 60, followed by a withdrawal of $68,897. At age 59, both accounts look decent. The Roth has $569,018 while the IUL has $739,258. However, the IUL started with a death benefit of over $400,000 on the first day and increased along with the cash value. This method is what we call "increasing" and it is best for the client.

After withdrawing $68,876 per year, the Roth IRA ran out of money by age 70, in just 10 years. Total accumulations over a 35-year period resulted in $210,000 in deposits and the account grew to $705,932, but all of it was gone by age 70. Total accumulations of $210,000 and withdrawing $705,932 looks great, but not when you compare it to the IUL.

On the other hand, the IUL was also set-up to withdraw the same amount of $68,897 between the ages of 60 and 90 years old. In this account, total withdrawals were $2,135,807. At the end of this time 67 years later, the IUL still has a strong cash value and a death benefit of $781,495. The cash value and the death benefit continued to grow. Clearly, the IUL is king.

For a 30-Year Old

The following chart shows the results of a 30-year-old contributing $1,000 per month into three different investment accounts. These accounts are a taxable account like a traditional IRA, 401(k), and 403(b), and two tax-free accounts. (Roth IRA and an IUL)

Comparison of 3 Investment Accounts for a 30-year Old (Figure 11.5)

| | | | IRA - 401k - 403b | | Roth IRA | | Index Universal Life (IUL) | | |
| | | | 1 Cash Withdrawal | 2 Account Value | 1 Cash Withdrawal | 2 Account Value | 1 Policy Loan | 2 Surrender Value | 3 Death Benefit |
Yr	Age	Deposit							
1	30	12.000	0	12.090	0	12.108	0	0	667.560
2	31	12.000	0	24.653	0	24.784	0	6.924	678.045
30	59	12.000		715876.000	0	787.051	0	960.065	1,617.752
		360.000			0		0		
31	60	0	100.380	694656.000	100.380	772.349	100.380	923.664	1,514.426
32	61	0	100.380	622409.000	100.380	706.960	100.380	886.619	1,405.46
40	69	0	6.660.000	0	100.380	45.153	100.380	574.546	878.930
41	70	0	0	0	45.153.000	0	100.380	534.467	840.190
61	90	0	0	0	0	0	100.380	132.051	535.739
62	91	0	0	0	0	0	0	261.824	607.311
		$ 360,000	$ 910,080		$ 1,048,953		$ 3,011,400		

Contributions of $1,000 per month end at age 60 and total contributions in all three accounts was $360,000. The distributions of $100,381 begin at age 61.

Notice that the taxable account (column 2) the funds last only until age 69. That is because the account is being taxed 15% when taken out. After age 69, this person has no money left in this taxable account.

In the third column, the Roth IRA account is a tax-free account and the money lasts until age 70, just one year longer. With the Roth IRA, this 30-year-old earned an extra $138,873, just enough for one more year of retirement funding.

However, looking at the IUL column on the right, this 30-year-old earned $3,011,400, almost 3 times the value of either the taxable accounts or the Roth IRA. In addition, with the IUL, this 30-year-old also received the value of a $607,311 death benefit as well, insuring his or her family are set in case of a tragedy. Any questions about which choice is the best one?

For a 45-Year Old

When it comes to investing for your future, time is of the essence. At age 45, there is less time before retirement so the contributions need to increase. In the following illustration, this individual is contributing $1,600 per month ($19,200 per year) until age 65 and receiving distributions of $44,089 per year after age 65.

The middle column shows the results for a taxable traditional IRA, a 401(k), or a 403(b). A tax rate of 15% was used in this example. As you can see, the taxable account runs out of money by age 95.

Comparison of a Taxable Account with an IUL for a 45-year Old (Figure 11.6)

Yr	Age	Deposit	IRA - Taxable		Index Universal Life (IUL)		
			1 Cash Withdrawal	2 Account Value	1 Cash Withdrawal	2 Surrender Value*	3 Death Benefit
1	45	19,200	0	20,223	0	288	516,038
2	46	19,200	0	41,524	0	17,964	532,927
20	64	19,200	0	692,468	0	655,024	1,155,024
21	65	0	44,089	682,934	44,089	653,142	1,153,142
50	94	0	44,089	22,030	44,089	853,371	1,353,371
51	95	0	22,030	0	44,089	846,921	1,346,921
52	96	0	0	0	44,089	833,967	1,333,967
53	97	0	0	0	44,089	814,093	1,314,093
54	98	0	0	0	44,089	783,099	1,283,099
55	99	0	0	0	44,089	741,788	1,241,788
56	100	0	0	0	44,089	702,232	1,202,232
57	101	0	0	0	0	704,528	1,204,528

Now take a look at the column on the right for the IUL. The IUL account continues paying annual distribution to age 100, and there is still $702,232 of cash value in the account and over $1.2 million in death benefits.

Full contributions in the taxable accounts were $384,000 ($19,200 x 20 years), and the distribution from the taxable accounts totaled $1,300,611.

Compared with the IUL which had the same contributions of $384,000, distributions from the IUL totaled $1,543,115 and included the big bonus of a death benefit for beneficiaries. If you are insurable, paying taxes now and opening an IUL might not be a bad idea. What do you think?

For a 60-Year Old (10 Years of Payments)

A 10-year pay is a very popular investment for people who have a large amount of money they wish to invest in an IUL or a Roth. Payments are withdrawn out of a 401(k) or an IRA. At age 59 ½ the 10% penalty is no longer a concern. Instead of converting these funds into a Roth IRA, the money could instead be converted into an IUL to obtain maximum benefits. The following chart demonstrates what happens when a 60-year-old deposits $100,000 into an IUL for 10 years, compared with a Roth IRA.

By paying $100,000 a year for 10 years, this 60-year-old made a $1 million total investment. In the middle column you can see that in a Roth IRA this account grew to $1,282,711 compared with the IUL in the column on the right which only grew to $1,097,686 over the course of 10 years.

Comparison of a Roth IRA Account with an IUL for a 60-year Old (Figure 11.7)

			Roth IRA		Index Universal Life (IUL)		
			1	2	1	2	3
			Cash	Account	Cash	Account	Death
Yr	Age	Deposit	Withdrawal	Value	Withdrawal	Value	Benefit
1	60	100,000	0	100,999	0	12,284	1,762,003
2	61	100,000	0	207,257	0	109,945	1,862,003
10	69	100,000	0	1,282,711	0	1,097,686	2,662,003
11	70	0	92,440	1,252,252	92,440	1,075,598	2,564,516
32	91	0	92,440	80,687	92,440	361,564	534,619
33	92	0	80,687	0	92,440	349,568	488,418
41	100	0	0	0	92,440	585,006	585,006
42	101	0	0	0	0	764,385	764,385

However, in Year 11, at age 70, the magic begins. Though both accounts make the same annual withdrawals of $92,440, the money in the Roth account is depleted by age 92. By comparison, the money in the IUL continues to age 100 and there is still a very large cash value and death benefit. What do you think? Are you convinced that IULs rule?

Conclusion

The preceding charts and distributions are just examples of what can be done to serve your financial future. There are many variations, and we can produce charts and illustrations to show what will happen with your unique circumstances when we customize a plan designed to specifically meet your retirement goals.

I believe you can see that these illustrations prove that at most ages, an IUL will produce significantly higher after-tax retirement funds than any qualified taxable plan, even performing better than a Roth IRA. All other investment options produce a lot less income, are usually drained too soon, and can be tragically affected by the unpredictable rise and fall of the stock market.

If you would like a free consultation to discuss your best options and view an illustration of your current financial situation, please let me know. I am certain I can increase your retirement income and help you reduce taxes in the future while preserving your wealth and keeping your money safe.

Summary

The lessons learned in this chapter are:

1. The Indexed Universal Life policy is possibly the best investment for you and your family's financial future.
2. Start an IUL account as soon as possible.
3. The length of investment time and the power of compound interest produce incredible results in an IUL.
4. My company offers a wide variety of investment products. We are happy to consider your financial needs and propose strategies that are perfectly suited for your portfolio's growth accumulation, wealth preservation, and retirement goals.

Chapter 12
Your Top 10 Questions ... Answered!

Many of our clients ask similar questions, so we have dedicated a chapter in this book to answer the most Frequently Asked Questions (FAQs) we receive. Perhaps you will find a question similar to your own that is answered from among those below.

Of course, we realize your question is specific to your own financial circumstances, and we welcome you giving us a call so we can talk about your unique situation and help you resolve your issue and secure your financial wealth.

FAQ #1: My Company provides a 401(k) and is matching 5% of my contributions. I am contributing 15% of my income every month. Right now, I have over $1 million in this 401(k) and $250,000 in a traditional IRA. I am 58 years old and thinking about retiring when I turn 60. What do you think I should do about future taxes?

Answer: First of all, congratulations! Your steady saving and investing over the years have turned into a tremendous asset for your retirement. My first piece of advice is not to wait until you retire to put together your retirement plan. Start now while there is time before you reach your chosen retirement age. This way you can organize and prepare so when you actually retire, your plan is already set-up and ready for you.

The second piece of advice is that we need to look at your tax status now and calculate what it will be when you turn 60. There are a number of tax saving strategies that can be implemented to reduce your taxes so you preserve more of your wealth. You might live a long time and you want your money to last, and maybe even provide a legacy for your loved ones.

My third piece of advice is to see if converting your traditional IRA into a Roth IRA is a good fit before the government raises the tax rate and you are forced to pay more taxes later than you will pay now at the lower tax rates.

FAQ #2: I've read your book and I'm interested in an Indexed Universal Life (IUL) policy. I'm 53 years old, so is it still financially sensible to convert my IRA into an IUL?

Answer: Yes, it still makes good financial sense to convert your traditional IRA into an IUL. However, you will have to pay taxes on the money in your traditional IRA, plus a 10% penalty for early withdrawal because you are not yet 59 ½ years old. Instead of converting your money in the traditional IRA into an IUL, a better tactic is to only convert your traditional IRA into a Roth IRA now.

Later, when you're 59 ½ or older, there is no penalty for converting into an IUL. In the meantime, if you don't have an IUL now, you should start one. This way you can begin building equity in your IUL right away and six years from now you can simply transfer the money in your Roth IRA into your IUL policy.

FAQ #3: I have a 401(k) account and an IRA, and I want to roll them over into a safe account. I also don't want to lose any growth potential. What I'm looking for is both security and growth. Is this possible?

Answer: Yes, this is possible. The choice I'd recommend for you is what I call a "hybrid index". It allows the company to reallocate the funds within the index to control volatility with zero risk.

Your account can also focus on safe accumulation with higher caps so your funds continue to grow. At the same, we can also see if an IUL could be an option for you. (See Figure 11.1)

FAQ #4: I am a father with a newborn child and my wife and I would like to get our baby girl started financially with an IRA. What do you suggest we do?

Answer: Congratulations on having a baby! If you really decide to have an IRA for her, you'll need to report income for her. However, instead of an IRA, you should start an Indexed Universal Life (IUL) policy for her.

The financial rewards are much higher. With an IUL you don't need to show income as long as you are in good health and you have life insurance yourself. In this book, I included an illustration comparing an IUL with a Roth IRA, and you can see how the IUL offers amazing results that the Roth IRA simply cannot match. Starting early is a great idea, and it's also inexpensive. (See Figure 11.3.)

FAQ #5: I noticed that you recommend taking loans from your IUL instead of withdrawing money. Please explain why loans are preferable to withdrawals.

Answer: This is one of the great benefits of having an IUL. When you make cash withdrawals, the money is permanently taken out of your cash value and won't earn any interest for you anymore. The money is gone. However, the benefit of having an IUL is that you can take a loan against your account's cash value and you will continue to earn interest on the money you are borrowing.

In other words, even though you are borrowing cash from your account, the money is still considered to be in your account. This way the money in your account, which includes the amount you are borrowing, is earning 6% - 9% average, but your cost for borrowing the money is less. This is a good debt to have because you're earning more interest than the interest you are paying for the loan. Your borrowed money is still earning interest for you, even though it's loaned to you.

FAQ #6: I have a pension, and I also have a traditional IRA. Should I stop my contributions to the traditional IRA and start a Roth IRA?

Answer: Yes, it's a good idea to start a Roth IRA. Since you have a taxable pension, having nontaxable accounts will help you manage your taxes in the future. Another idea is to convert your traditional IRA into a Roth IRA now because the tax rates are still low. They won't be low much longer so this is a good time to act. I recommend you speak with your income tax preparer to make sure this is a good idea for your unique circumstances.

FAQ #7: I wish to invest $20,000 per year in a Roth IRA but there are annual limits. What are my options?

Answer: That's true, there are annual limits on how much money you can contribute to an IRA. If you are under 50 years old, your maximum amount is $6,000, and $7,000 if you are older than 50. If you are married, one option is to open both a Roth IRA and a traditional IRA each for you and your wife. You can convert the traditional IRA into a Roth IRA later. A second option is to open an IUL because an IUL is also tax-free and allows you to contribute even higher amounts of money when the policy is designed properly. (See Figure 11.5)

FAQ #8: I like what I've been learning about IULs. They seem good investment vehicles and I'd like to get one, but I don't think I'm insurable. What can I do?

Answer: I recommend you apply for an IUL anyway. There is no cost to do so. I've noticed that companies are more lenient now than before and you might get a really nice surprise. If you want the IUL for investment purposes, I strongly recommend you get one for your wife and/or your children. They can be the named insured, and you can be the owner and keep full control of the account.

FAQ #9: I have a 403(b) at work, like many of my friends. They all think it's a great investment for retirement, but I've been hearing this may not be so. What do you think?

Answer: A 403(b) has some good features, but it is not as strong a retirement investment as other products you can choose. Unlike a 401(k), your employer is not contributing matching funds to your account. An IRA has more control. Also, your 403(b) has higher fees than other similar investment products. I suggest you start a tax-free account to maintain a balance in your retirement portfolio. I recommend you try a Roth IRA, and I definitely suggest you look into starting an IUL. I can help you transition to any of these investments. Give this book to your friends to read. (See Figure 11.5.)

FAQ #10: Since I already have life insurance, do you think I should get a Roth IRA instead of an IUL?

Answer: This is a matter of preference. Of the many people I advise and help, after seeing the comparisons, most of them prefer the IUL as an investment, not for the insurance. I teach my clients to buy the least amount of insurance with the maximum premium so the difference between the two is invested in their ever-growing cash value. Remember, another huge benefit is that the money in your IUL account is tax-free when withdrawn, which is a huge bonus for people in retirement.

Summary

The lesson learned in this chapter is:

Everybody has their own unique questions and concerns. They either don't have enough invested for retirement or they have no idea what they have. Everybody needs a personalized life or annuity policy review in order to better understand their personal situation.

Conclusion
Build and Preserve Your Wealth ...
Start Today!

Am I going to have enough money for retirement? Did I invest enough? Did I make the right decisions? Are taxes going to be an issue? How do I protect myself from market volatility? We help our clients answer these questions and create a plan to help everybody address all these different concerns. We can help you make changes to obtain a happy and a stress free retirement.

The message is clear. We are currently enjoying historically low tax rates. Our nation is in a very difficult time economically with the constantly increasing burden of Baby Boomers drawing their Social Security benefits, entering Medicare, and the recent economic disaster of COVID-19. Our government cannot stop spending.

Congress will be forced to increase taxes which means that the lifestyle you've planned for yourself in retirement is at risk. We have a tax problem. We have a deficit problem. And teachers in the TRS system have an even bigger problem than taxes to worry about.

You can't fix the US deficit nor the TRS system but you can try to fix your own personal accounts to avoid over-taxation in the future. Now is the time to make the necessary changes that will preserve your financial wealth and protect you from taxes. How many times have you said, "If I would have known about that 20 years ago..." or "I should have bought Apple Stocks." In this situation, you know now and you can start now, not only for you but for your family.

It doesn't matter if you are a Doctor, Lawyer, Real Estate Agent or a Teacher, we have the solutions to guide you with your present accounts or to start a tax-free retirement plan.

If you are like most people, you have lazy money sitting in your bank in a CD or money market account where you are losing value daily as inflation eats away at your funds.

You may have an old annuities, 401(k) or an IRA that should be transferred to the newer and better performing accounts available today. At the same time, you can avoid market risk or perhaps convert your account now to avoid taxes in the future. Whatever you have now, you owe it to yourself and your family to look into tax-free accounts and avoid market risk without sacrificing growth. The truth is that most people feel they are okay and don't realize the importance of time and the magic of compounding.

By now we all have seen the commercials that say, "Just okay is not okay". Or maybe you remember the phrase "Good enough never is". When it comes to your retirement and your family's future, just being okay is never good enough.

Whatever your age is and whatever type of account you have now, allow us to give you a free policy review. You have seen different illustrations on fixed index annuities, Roth and IULs that average 6% - 9% with guarantees of never losing any of the money in your accounts. We'll provide a no-obligation illustration so you can have a clear idea about what your financial future could look like. This will take just a few minutes and it is completely free. The sooner we work on your retirement goals the happier you would be doing your retirement. Hopefully this book helped you answered most of your questions.

Special Offer from Cayetano

People often ask me, "Hey, Cayetano, what should I do next?"

First, schedule your first consultation to review what you presently have in your retirement portfolio.

It's a great opportunity, and here are my three promises:

Number One: I'm usually going to be able to uncover at least two opportunities to either increase your income or reduce your taxes.

Number Two: We are going to use computerized illustrations that will compare the different products and scenarios that will allow you to make a wise decision.

Number Three: All decisions are yours to make. We will simply advise you about all the possible outcomes that will benefit you and your family. These recommendations will be based on your personal needs and not the agent's.

Learn ways to increase your retirement income tax-free while keeping your money safe, and without losing any growth potential. Let's see if we can move some or all of those taxable accounts into tax-free accounts.

If you would like to schedule your Tactical Retirement Consultation, give me a call at 844-827-7296 or 956-685-5181.

I'd love to speak with you and your family and I'm ready for your call.

Best wishes!

Made in the USA
Columbia, SC
16 August 2020